A Chime of Words

To my friend with the with best wishes R

A Chime
of Words

THE LETTERS OF
LOGAN PEARSALL SMITH

·

EDITED BY EDWIN TRIBBLE
FOREWORD BY JOHN RUSSELL

TICKNOR & FIELDS · NEW YORK

1984

Frontispiece: Watercolor of Logan Pearsall Smith by
Sir William Rothenstein
Passages from *Afterthoughts, All Trivia,* and *Unforgotten Years*
are quoted with the kind permission of John Russell.
"To Logan Pearsall Smith," on page 120, is quoted from
The Collected Works of Robert C. Trevelyan, published by
Longmans, Green & Company, Ltd., London, 1939.

Library of Congress Cataloging in Publication Data

Smith, Logan Pearsall, 1865–1946.
A chime of words.

Includes index.
1. Smith, Logan Pearsall, 1865–1946 — Correspondence.
2. Authors, English — 20th century — Correspondence.
3. Authors, American — 20th century — Correspondence.
I. Tribble, Edwin. II. Title.
PR6037.M5Z48   1984   828'.91209 [B]   83–18010
ISBN 0–89919–232–7

Printed in the United States of America

V 10 9 8 7 6 5 4 3 2 1

Two weeks before Logan's death a friend asked him half-jokingly if he had discovered any meaning in life. "Yes," he replied, "there is a meaning, at least for me, there is one thing that matters — to set a chime of words tinkling in the minds of a few fastidious people."

— Cyril Connolly
in the *New Statesman and Nation,*
March 9, 1946

Contents

Foreword

BY JOHN RUSSELL

To a degree not often rivaled, Logan Pearsall Smith lived for letters. Past letters, present letters, letters thought out but not yet set down — all were a joy to him.

During the long period that he lived in London, the Royal Mails acted as his accomplice. Four times a day the postman came to call. He was there before breakfast. He was there before lunch. He was there at tea-time. He was there before dinner. Those were quiet years along St. Leonard's Terrace, and you could hear the postman's peremptory rat-a-tat-tat a hundred yards away. To one who lived for letters there was something thrilling about the steady crescendo of that rat-a-tat-tat, and when at last the young stalwart bounded up the steps of No. 11 and shook the whole house with his knocking there could be no doubt whatever that a new batch of letters had arrived.

They came from all over — from George Santayana in Rome, from the Berensons outside Florence, from scholar gypsies in France and Germany and Spain, from editors and publishers and aspirant writers in the United States of America, and from the ladies of high degree in London and elsewhere whom Logan feigned to mock. Japanese readers, loyal then as now to his book on "The English Language," were always after him. Word-men of all nationalities were after him, in fact, and so were readers of *All Trivia* in this language or that. There were old friendships to be kept in repair, and new ones to be nurtured, and one of the more persistently verbal of recorded families to be kept up with. The country that had institutionalized among much else the office of Writer to the Signet should also have created the office of Postman to Mr. Pearsall Smith.

The love of letters had always been with him. His immediate relations — mother, sisters, brothers-in-law, nephews and nieces, cousins beyond number — were all correspondents. (Mary Berenson is believed to have written well over two million words in her letters, and that figure is likely to fall short of the truth.) Logan himself began early, stepped up the rhythm when he was on his own in Europe, and never stopped. He was to the day of his death the man who once said that "People say that life is the thing, but I prefer reading"; and he preferred reading letters to reading almost anything else.

Doubtless it helped that he had nothing much else to do. From time to time he had great endeavors under way, and from time to time he gave of his very best within the compass of the essay. His book of memoirs, *Unforgotten Years,* though far from confidential, is a remarkable record not only of a vanished age but of an attitude of mind now rarely met with. But letters were what kept his enormous old head ticking and caused his massive old limbs to make the short journey across the room to the complete Oxford English Dictionary and back again to the armchair that overlooked the trophied gates, the decorous playing fields, and the profile of Sir Christopher Wren's Chelsea Hospital.

He knew how lucky he was. "Now all my days are Sundays," he once wrote. And his days indeed were his own to order, and there were seven of them every week, and never did anyone interfere with his adjustment of them. Barely had he got to France, close on a hundred years ago, than he chose Flaubert as his "saint and hero." It was not for the novels that he revered Flaubert primarily, but for his stance before life, and more specifically for his letters, of which only four volumes had then appeared. "The four volumes of his letters were like a Bible to me," he wrote later, "and now, when I look at the texts I marked, the old flames illuminate those pages."

Later, when he began to write the life of the poet, ambassador, and Provost of Eton, Sir Henry Wotton (1568–1639), it was in transcribing Wotton's unpublished letters that he found a supreme satisfaction. In one spectacular instance (and in one of the biggest houses in England) he found not only unpublished letters of Wotton's but unpublished letters of John Donne's also.

"Seek, and ye shall find" is a maxim that applies particularly to the letter-hound, and Logan never forgot the part that he played in the unearthing of "hundreds and hundreds of unpublished letters from Madame du Deffand, who was only second in fame as a letter-writer to Madame de Sévigné. They were all annotated (evidently for publication) by Horace Walpole himself. Among them were a certain number of Walpole's own letters, though he seems to have destroyed most of them on account of the bad French in which he believed that they had been written." That is what it means to live for letters.

Letters were for Logan Pearsall Smith the very perfection of human exchange. Often separated from the people he liked best, and subject to recurrent fits of depression that made it difficult for him to maintain an easy, even tenor in everyday life, he became his best self as soon as pens, ink, and paper were before him. As a letter-writer he was generous with his time, his affection, and his superabundant curiosity. Letter-writing sharpened his perceptions, deepened his insights, and quickened his memory. Almost until the end of his life, age and infirmity dropped away when he sat down to write a letter. At that moment he was one with Madame de Sévigné, on whom he wrote in 1926 what is still the best brief study in English. He was one with Thomas Carlyle, two hundred and fifty-seven of whose unpublished letters he once tracked down. And he was one with Edward FitzGerald, whose letters (and whose range of acquaintance) had much in common with his own.

As to what came of it, readers can judge for themselves. But I shall be surprised if they do not agree with what Logan Pearsall Smith says somewhere in this book — that "fine things are all the finer for being a while forgotten."

Introduction

Within the strict limits he set for himself, Logan Pearsall Smith was one of the finest writers of his time. A man who cherished words and loved the music of prose, Smith described his art as "transfixing the ignominies of our nature onto the pins of polished phrases." His readers expected small perfections from him in his books of aphorisms, essays, and criticism, and they were not disappointed; if they wanted deep and alarming things — interminable novels, long histories, or detailed treatises — they turned to others. Smith's books are few but they are classics of their kind and the number of them still in print shows that they have not faded entirely from memory. There have always been readers who go back to them with pleasure; they are zealous and, while perhaps not numerous, they are loyal.

The book for which he is best remembered hides behind a falsely modest title, *All Trivia*. It is a collection of wise and witty comments on life and letters, "short pithy statements containing truths of general import," as the dictionary requires of aphorisms. Smith's own definition of the word is more creative:

Aphorisms [he wrote in the Introduction to his *A Treasury of English Aphorisms*] are no flights of fancy, no fruits culled from the Hesperian gardens of the imagination; they are products of the familiar earth, and smack of the world we live in. They cover the whole field of practical experience, from the lowest maxims of shop-keeping prudence to the

[xiii]

highest rules of conduct; and our knowledge of ourselves and others, of the human heart and its springs of action, of love and hate and envy and ambition, of the characters and manners of mankind, of all the weaknesses and follies and absurdities of human nature, is embodied and stored up in this immense accumulation of wise observations. . . . This gnomic wisdom, it has been said, is the true salt of literature, and those books, at least in prose, are most nourishing which are most saturated with it.

Smith's own aphorisms are sometimes only a sentence, sometimes a paragraph or two, and very infrequently, a short narrative. All are the original and stimulating thoughts of an articulate and enlightened man. The first ones were printed privately in 1902 in a little book called *Trivia*. More came in succeeding years — at rare intervals, for they could not be done in a hurry — and finally, in 1933, they were collected in *All Trivia*.

There were other books, too. A few years later came *Unforgotten Years,* about his boyhood, youth, and early middle age. This short book brought Smith his first large public, mingling his particular brand of fastidiousness with the mass appeal of the Book-of-the-Month Club, which distributed it in America. It was an association that both surprised and chagrined him since he had not expected the book to have mass appeal. His longest work was a two-volume life of a man who was not rescued from obscurity even by Smith's scholarly attention. He was Sir Henry Wotton, a seventeenth-century British diplomat and poet who was the author of that inspired definition of an ambassador as "an honest man sent to lie abroad for the good of his country."

Smith also tried poetry and fiction, but only long enough to prove to himself that his talent lay in essays and criticism. He wrote about Shakespeare and Milton, whose greatness constantly awed him, and about Jeremy Taylor and Fulke Greville, who satisfied his lifelong fascination with the obscure. There were also books on the English language — words and idioms and fine writing — some of them still read, and all of them designed to delight those who are not content merely to read good prose but want to know what makes it good.

Smith spent a long life — he lived to be eighty — in the pursuit of knowledge and the perfect phrase. He labored over his books and improved them as they were reprinted (he once said he hoped God was not a collector of first editions). Although his large family had deep roots in America they preferred to live abroad, and it was in England that Smith wrote all his books and most of his letters. Other members of the family were ardent correspondents, and while he had the reputation among them of being the one who never wrote, it must be said that this reputation was entirely relative: by any normal standards he was a prolific writer of letters. Entertaining, instructive, and often moving, the letters are even more original and stimulating than his books. Smith's comments on the death of Henry James, for example, are surely among the finest tributes ever paid to that constantly praised man. A few of his letters appeared in memoirs written after his death; many more of them are collected here for the first time.

*   *   *

Smith was the product of an austere American Quakerism. His earliest ancestor in this country, a Scotsman named James Logan, came to Pennsylvania in the seventeenth century as secretary to William Penn. A generation or two later, Smith's grandfather married into an equally strong Quaker family from Long Island, the Pearsalls, who provided the family with, among other things, a much-used middle name. Plain living and sober thinking made the Pearsall Smiths conspicuous for public service and civic responsibility. Of equally unimpeachable Quaker credentials were the Whitalls of New Jersey, and when young Robert Pearsall Smith married Hannah Whitall in 1851 it was a marriage of the most promising kind. Hannah brought even higher standards of intellectuality, morality, and missionary zeal, and while none of the family would have put it just that way, she also brought a financial independence that enabled them to pursue their aims in life without the necessity of earning a living.

John Whitall, Hannah's father, had run away as a boy and sharpened his instinct for trade by watching the world at work in foreign ports. Returning home, he started a manufacturing business, which, because of the insatiable demand for glass bottles, prospered greatly and became the source of his fortune. He was uncomfortable in his prosperity, however, and in 1865 he retired, saying he felt he had made enough money and that he intended to spend the rest of his life in good works. This he did.

Hannah Whitall quickly established herself as the dominant member of her new Smith family in Philadelphia; her husband went to work for her father; the family grew. Robert was sent to a small town in New Jersey called Millville and it was there, on October 18, 1865, that their fourth child, Logan Pearsall Smith, was born.

Hannah and Robert were deeply religious but they found they could not accept their Society of Friends heritage with its emphasis on the corruption of man and the prospect of doom, and by the time they went to Millville they were experimenting with new beliefs and practices, their own version of "The Higher Life." They were swept into a wave of revivalism: impassioned preaching in camp meetings, public professions of faith, and an almost physical exaltation in the experience of salvation. Their new faith and conversion gave them forgiveness for their sins and allowed them a baptism of the spirit by which they reached Sanctification. This religion — unorganized for the most part — owed something to the various evangelical faiths, Baptists, Methodists, and Presbyterians, but it had its own individuality and it became known as the Holiness movement.

Hannah and Robert, devout and energetic and with time at their disposal, were destined to be more than mere communicants, and soon they were preaching. Robert, a handsome, emotional man, was the convincing advocate who swayed the crowds, and Hannah, more intellectual, was the force that held things together. Her heresies (she did not, for example, believe in eternal punishment) were on the human side and she quickly won a personal following.

The Smiths did not stay in Millville long. In 1868, when Logan was three years old, they returned to Philadelphia. There were six children in all but only three grew to maturity: Logan; Mary, a year older; and Alys, two years younger. Servants and relatives took care of the children while Robert and Hannah preached and wrote religious tracts. Logan recalled that in his childhood they lived in constant expectation of the Day of Judgment. But it was not long before the family encountered its first trouble: Robert's health failed and he went away for treatment for a nervous breakdown. When he came back it was to devote all his time to preaching and to a new religious paper he had started, *The Christian's Pathway to Power*. It was soon clear that he was not well enough to continue and a vacation trip to Egypt was planned to spur his recovery. He got as far as England, where he found a new wave of evangelism that appealed to him, doctrines of salvation he understood. Its leaders, friends of his father's, were eager to welcome him and to hear his message. He was successful from the start, the converts were even more ardent than the Americans, and their testimonials to personal salvation were even more stirring. They poured their resources (which were considerable, for they were almost all rich) into winning souls for Christ. Hannah contributed to the cause in 1875 by publishing an inspirational book, *The Christian's Secret of a Happy Life*. It became one of the most popular religious books of all time; millions of copies have been sold and it is still in print.

Hannah was no less successful as a preacher. She and Robert spent much of their time in England. Both Mary and Alys wanted an education; Mary went to Smith College and then to the Harvard Annex (later Radcliffe) and Alys was in the first class at the new Bryn Mawr at Philadelphia. As for Logan, he had been a late developer; he did not learn to read until he was ten, an amazing fact in the light of his lifelong devotion to books. He was sent to outdoor camps in the West to develop a physical sturdiness that never came, but most of his early schooling was in the Friends' William Penn Charter School in Philadelphia. In 1881, when he was sixteen, he was enrolled at Haverford College.

By this time the parents were making regular trips to England and to the Continent, where Robert's fame had spread and where he led highly successful crusades in Germany, Switzerland, France, Holland, and Belgium. Hannah joined him and their work was at its peak when a shattering blow fell: Robert was accused of taking a more than Christian interest in one of his women followers, and the close relationship between the spiritual and the physical sides of their religion was subjected to an unwelcome examination. Robert protested his innocence, but his preaching career was ruined by the gossip. He went back to Philadelphia, lost his faith, and quit the ministry. Hannah supported her husband throughout the ordeal, but kept to her religious mission with zeal and their ties to England grew even stronger.

In 1885 Mary married Frank Costelloe, a young Irish barrister. The ceremony was at Oxford and attracted many university scholars, the most awesome being Benjamin Jowett, master of Balliol College. Logan was present, too, and the day was a turning point in his life; he resolved to go to Oxford himself someday. He had left Haverford, had spent a year at Harvard as a special student, and was now en route to Germany for further study. He had promised to work for the family business when his year in Germany was over, and in the fall of 1886 he went into the New York offices of Whitall, Tatum and Company, where he soon discovered that he had no talent for trade and that he could not get Oxford out of his mind. Frank Costelloe arranged for him to go to Balliol, and Logan talked his family into giving him the money. So, in the fall of 1888, he sailed from New York for England. He remained there for the rest of his life.

Not long after Logan's departure, the rest of his family decided to live in England themselves. Mary Costelloe and her husband were in London with their two young daughters, Ray, born in 1887, and Karin, in 1889. Robert and Hannah established themselves in a country house called Friday's Hill, forty-five miles from London in a village called Fernhurst, near Haslemere, on the Sussex downs. A large, ivy-clad brick building, the house had fourteen bedrooms, all of which were usually occupied. There were tennis courts and a conservatory and a smoking room — desite Quaker disapproval of the habit. There was a literary tradition in the Haslemere countryside: George Eliot had lived nearby, and later Alfred Tennyson and numerous other writers had lived there. Friday's Hill under Hannah's hospitality became a gathering place for friends the Smiths had met in their religious work, many of them titled, and, it seemed, all anxious to spread the word that a new religion was enriching their lives.

The atmosphere was by no means entirely religious: George Bernard Shaw and Beatrice and Sidney Webb were there arguing their Fabian Socialist views, William Rothenstein and Roger Fry talked about art, and William James and George Santayana talked about everything. As Logan recalled the scene: "A summer colony for discussing the world in general was assembled on the terrace all day long. I don't know that we came to any conclusions different from the old one that the world is a funny place."

The family of Lord John Russell, the famous prime minister, lived nearby, and before long Bertrand, the young grandson of the statesman, was paying court to Alys, whom he married in 1894. Mary Costelloe brought into the circle a young man just out of Harvard who changed her life. Bernard Berenson was starting a career that was to make him the leading authority on Italian Renaissance painting. Mary left her husband to go to Florence with him, and after they were married in 1900, they established I Tatti, the Tuscan villa that is now the Harvard University Center for Renaissance Studies. In time, Mary's daughter Ray Costelloe married Oliver Strachey, younger brother of Lytton Strachey, and her other daughter, Karin, married Adrian Stephen, younger brother of Virginia Woolf, and thus those two famous Bloomsbury families were also brought into the Friday's Hill circle.

The sophistication of Haslemere did not, however, diminish Hannah's search for a better world. She intensified her work for two causes: the Women's Christian Temperance Union and the Woman's Suffrage Movement. She spoke at innumerable meetings, toured America with British reformers decrying the evils of drink and the injustice of disfranchisement, and still had time to revise her *Christian's Secret* and to write other books with such titles as *The Way to Be Holy* and *The Unselfishness of God*.

Leaving Oxford in 1891 with a bachelor of arts degree, Logan went to Paris to become a writer. He took part in the expatriate life in the Latin Quarter, met Whistler, and walked the boulevards, but by the end of 1895, and after extensive travels in other countries, he was back in England. He leased a farmhouse called High Buildings, near Haslemere, and took up the life of an English country gentleman of literary ambitions. Compton Mackenzie, who was later famous as a novelist, met him then, described him as "a thin man with a sharp nose and seeming by the way he kept peering about him with fidgety gestures to be short-sighted." He was large in frame, with a slight stoop, and his movements were quick.

Smith had written six short stories in Paris, which he collected into his first book, *The Youth of Parnassus*, published in 1895. All of the stories were about life in Oxford and in later years he described them as "labored, imitative, and rather lifeless." They made little impression on the public although the reviews were generally polite.

By the time of his return to England Smith was already at work on the Wotton biography, but it would be ten years before he finished it. Meanwhile, the notes he was jotting down on everything that came into his head became *Trivia*. The form was random; he thought of it as "musical prose, without rhythm or rhyme, supple and abrupt enough to express the sudden joy of the spirit, the undulations of our reveries . . . composed like a book of verses, of loosely connected and disconnected fragments, each piece having a life of its own." If Maupassant was the model for his short stories (and Smith said he was), the notes he was now making were inspired by Baudelaire.

The *Trivia* pieces were ignored or scorned as inconsequential when they were published in a very small edition in 1902. Later they won gradual and wide acceptance and they are now considered the most lasting accomplishment of their author. There were always a few detractors who complained that they were bloodless and overbred and would have preferred the larger reflections of a coarser writer, but most readers respected the author's right to his own style. Christopher Morley, the American novelist and critic, thought of them this way: "How would you describe a vintage wine, say a Musigny? or a dogwood tree in its autumnal purple-orange? or a *leitmotiv* in music? or a sudden stricture of night-waking misery? . . . Whether of irony or mischief, pathos or euphoria, each perfectly outlines — and communicates — an emotion, a social comedy, or an all-too-human horror."

Smith's writings were never rushed into print. It was five years after *Trivia* that the book on Wotton appeared from the Oxford University Press, marking the beginning of a long and happy association with that publisher. It has remained the standard biography of Wotton, and the numerous references to it in Smith's letters show his pride in being accepted as a writer of scholarly attainments. In 1909 came his only book of poems, *Songs and Sonnets.* They were lyrics of slight content and he was the first to admit that he was no rival of his friend and Oxford neighbor, Robert Bridges, the poet laureate.

In these years Smith leased various places at Oxford but kept his country house at Haslemere, where his mother lived with him after the death of Robert in 1898 caused her to give up Friday's Hill. She herself died in 1911 and Alys moved in with her brother, her marriage to Bertrand Russell having ended in separation that year.

About this time Smith produced one of his shortest but most enduring books, *The English Language,* published in 1912 and still in print. In it, Smith discusses words as though they were historical documents, thereby producing one of the best and most succinct histories of our language. The subject was the one closest to the author — the language itself. It fascinated him all his life, and he made his own study of the styles of many writers. An idea of his method may be found in his comments on the seventeenth-century writer Jeremy Taylor, one of his particular favorites. He described the things he liked best in Taylor's style as "the sound and the image, the verbal music which enchants the ear and the picture which fascinates the eye . . . a felicity of sound and rhythm."

In the Introduction to *The Golden Grove,* his collection of quotations from Taylor, he shed this light on the author's style:

This wonder-working effect of sound and rhythm can perhaps be best noted when Jeremy Taylor expresses the same idea in a less, and then a more perfect form. Thus in one of his earlier works he writes, "Lucifer and many Angels walking across the battlements of heaven grew top-heavy and fell into the state of devils"; but in the *Holy Dying* he says of these fallen angels, "They grew vertiginous and fell from the battlements of Heaven." In the contrast of these phrases, they "grew top-heavy and fell into the state of devils" — "they grew vertiginous and fell from the battlements of Heaven," we can perceive the little changes of sound and rhythm which make so much difference — and how much it is! Another instance may be given. In one passage Jeremy Taylor compares the death of virtuous men to the "descending of ripe and wholesome fruits from a pleasant and florid tree," but in another to "ripe and pleasant fruit falling from a fair tree and gathered into baskets for the planter's use." Here again, with just a slight change of cadence, a new arrangement of epithets, the miracle happens, the crystallization takes place, and the phrase becomes a phrase of enchantment.

Smith quoted many of Taylor's passages about nature, but he seldom wrote about it himself; human conduct and books interested him most. "I wasn't made for the world of granite and iron and hunger we are living in now," he once wrote, "it's too grim and serious and forbidding. I want a world with hammocks and sunshine and delphiniums and talk and exquisitely improper French novels." This was, of course, a facetious remark; he cared deeply about all written words.

* * *

In 1914 Smith moved into the London townhouse where he lived until he died more than thirty years later. No. 11 St. Leonard's Terrace is a narrow six-story stucco house, one of a row, facing the grounds of the Royal Hospital of Chelsea. Smith fitted so naturally into Chelsea, with its literary and artistic history, that it is difficult to imagine him living anywhere else. When he became known, inevitably, as "the sage of Chelsea," he submitted with the proper protestations but it was an appropriate if overused title. He worked hard through the years on the books he produced while he lived there, polishing and repolishing, writing and discarding, and he spent countless hours engaged in his "unpunished vice," reading. He liked to keep his friends and correspondents advised about what he was reading and thus it is that we have such startling news that at one time during his own period of greatest writing activity he was also going through the seventy volumes of Thomas Carlyle. His taste for the sermons and miscellaneous writings of early churchmen — nearly all of whom were extremely verbose — consumed many hours.

Among Smith's friends were many in London's writing world — authors, editors, critics, publishers, the ambitious and struggling as well as the established. His good talk had a proper setting in his book-filled rooms, and several generations of writers came to feel at home there, talking about books, getting ideas for books of their own, and exchanging mock-insults with Smith over their borrowing habits. Titled ladies of leisure and culture with tart tongues were charmed by him; he called them his Mayfair Jezebels and went to all their parties. Virginia Woolf described him in her *Diary* for May 18, 1919:

> Logan does his turns which take the form of "delightful adventures — life is like the Arabian Nights" — & good stories, quotations & recitations . . . He is a very well brushed, bright eyed, rosy cheeked man, seemingly entirely satisfied with life, which he appears to have mastered; visiting each of its flowers like a bee. These flowers he keeps stored in his waistcoat pocket: lines from Jeremy Taylor, Carlyle, and Lamb etc. An Epicurean, I suppose; a little frosty, I conjecture, though kindly and humane of course rather than human.

A procession of young men served as secretary-apprentices, relieving him of research on the essays he wrote and later published in book form, and preparing bibliographies for the six anthologies he edited. Cyril Connolly, the brightest man in his class at Oxford, was the first assistant, and then for seventeen years there was Robert Gathorne-Hardy, a young aristocrat whose association with Smith ended in an estrangement not long before his death. As he grew older Smith suffered alternating periods of elation and depression which affected his ability to work and led occasionally to illnesses.

> I am what is called a depressive manic [he wrote in 1941], a victim of periods of ecstasy and euphorics in the spring and summer, followed by months of dullness and depression in the autumn when I am almost incapable of speech and take not the slightest pleasure in the sight of people or gaggle of human beings. I read history in these periods and the time passes dully but not too unpleasantly if I am left alone. It is a curious alternation of two forms of insanity, in the euphoric stage I write blackmailing letters, lovely prose, am incapable of any misdemeanor (as you may have noticed). In the period underground I am intensely dull and moral and in consequence boring beyond endurance.

He suffered a particularly severe attack in 1938 while on a trip to Iceland with Gathorne-Hardy. He was taken to a hospital and nearly died, and his obituaries were published in New York newspapers, to his vast and unending amusement. Though he recovered and returned to London, he remained irrational for a long time. Gathorne-Hardy wrote a book, *Recollections of Logan Pearsall Smith: The Story of a Friendship*, to describe this and other experiences with a man of so many troubles and also of so many rewards.

There were other disciples. Kenneth Clark was an early one, and he and his wife Jane were both favorites. Desmond MacCarthy and Raymond Mortimer were also friends and became, with Cyril Connolly, the best British literary critics of their time. Hugh Trevor-Roper came at the beginning of the Second World War, and it was to him that Smith wrote a remarkable series of letters revealing his mental vitality in his last years. John Russell met him in 1942 through a mutual friend and began under Smith's admiring eye the career that led to many books, to twenty-seven years on the staff of the *London Sunday Times,* and eventually to the *New York Times,* where he is now chief art critic.

* * *

Smith was seventy-five at the outbreak of the Second World War. The unexpected success of *Unforgotten Years* in 1939 had made him famous, and his books of essays and his anthologies had slowly attracted the kind of following that he had always wanted — highly literate, often academic, and a little remote from the marketplace of popular writers. His life at St. Leonard's Terrace pleased him: Alys still lived with him and she had made a busy life for herself working for numerous good causes. A housekeeper and a cook made life pleasant for them. There were royalties from *Unforgotten Years* (and, by now, from *All Trivia*), but for the first time money became a matter of concern, due in part to war-time restrictions, which were complicated by the fact that Smith had, in 1913, become a British subject. There had always been an income from trust funds in the United States and in an earlier and happier time he had written to one correspondent, Philip Morrell, this joking account of how he got his money:

> What a joy it is to be hot and leisurely with a lot of people to work for you! I can never get over the charming injustice and absurdity of it. Just out of pedantry and convention, it is agreed that I have money and other people haven't. There is a large room in London with great glass doors, and there behind a counter sits a grave-faced bearded man, who bows to me when I go in, and hands me out gold in a brass shovel, with a bow.

No. 11 St. Leonard's Terrace was hit several times in air raids during the war. Smith was properly stoical and refused to leave, but his health grew worse under the strain. He wrote *Milton and His Modern Critics,* a short book to show his scorn for T. S. Eliot and Ezra Pound, who had consistently criticized Milton as obscure in meaning, turgid in expression, and needlessly involved in syntax. Smith's defense of

[xxv]

the great poet was done with a cutting wit, and critics loved the sight of an old writer getting the best in an argument. Published in 1941, it was the last book he wrote.

His friends continued to visit during the war, and every now and then an American soldier came to his door with his young head filled with quotations from *All Trivia,* and he would think it had all been worthwhile. The London critics still sought his advice respectfully, and his ideas showed up in their reviews. The Library of Congress wrote to ask for his manuscripts to add to its collection of papers of important American writers. He talked to his visitors about books he had never written, especially the one on the man he admired most of all, Henry James. He sat on a bench in front of his house and chatted with all and sundry. Having never found the solace in religion that had so sustained his mother, he now grew more philosophical in his letters. Those to Kenneth Clark and to Hugh Trevor-Roper show that he knew his time was running out, although he never failed to joke about it. The end of the war in 1945 gave him much relief, but by the fall he was ill again. He seemed better after Christmas but the improvement did not last, and he died on March 2, 1946, in his bedroom at 11 St. Leonard's Terrace.

* * *

"His going leaves an unfillable gap," wrote Rose Macaulay, in *Time and Tide,* March 9, "His was the kind of ripe and scholarly culture that links yesterday (not today) with past centuries; he was at home with the great *littérateurs,* French and English, of the Nineteenth century, the Eighteenth, and (pre-eminently) the Seventeenth. Whenever and wherever men and women have made beauty out of words, there was his quarry. The scholar in him led him to track down and dig out of the lairs, where unheeding owners had left them to moulder, manuscripts of priceless value to students, as when he dug up an undiscovered volume of Sir Henry Wotton's papers in the neglected lumber room of an oblivious colonel. It was partly the scholar too, that quested after curious and beautiful words, collecting them like coins; but it was the artist and stylist who delighted in fashioning out

[xxvi]

of them mosaics of lovely color and pattern. For he was, of course, first and last a stylist; his aim from youth was to 'master the powers of magical evocation, the elfin music, the ironic echoes which are latent in English prose. The golden sceptre of style gilds everything it touches and can make immortal those who grasp it.' So he wrote in one of his most characteristic essays, his tract on Fine Writing."

Acknowledgments

I am deeply indebted to John Russell, friend of Logan Pearsall Smith and holder of the rights to his writings, for permission to make this selection and for his unfailing help and enthusiasm in its preparation. This book includes letters from his *A Portrait of Logan Pearsall Smith Drawn from His Letters and Diaries,* published in a limited edition by the Dropmore Press in London in 1950, and from his large collection of unpublished Smith family letters.

Barbara Strachey Halpern, Smith's great-niece, kindly opened to me the Pearsall Smith family archives that she keeps in her house in Oxford, and many of the letters are from there. For these and for information about the family I am grateful. I have also found helpful her book, *Remarkable Relations: The Story of the Pearsall Smith Family,* published in England by Victor Gollancz in 1980 and in the United States by Universe Books in 1982.

Hugh Trevor-Roper, Lord Dacre of Glanton, generously allowed me to use the remarkable letters Smith wrote to him in the last years of his life, a copious correspondence filled with the mature wisdom of the author.

The Jane and Kenneth Clark letters are used with the permission of the late Lord Clark of Saltwood, one of Smith's most treasured friends.

The Helen Thomas Flexner letters are from the Flexner papers at the American Philosophical Society and are used with the permission of the Society and James Thomas Flexner.

The Robert Gathorne-Hardy letters appeared originally in his *Recollections* of Smith and are reproduced here through the courtesy of his literary heir, Jonathan Gathorne-Hardy.

The originals of the Bertrand Russell letters are in the library of the MacMaster University in Hamilton, Ontario; and Carl Spadoni, assistant archivist there, was helpful in guiding me to other Smith letters as well. The letters to Russell appeared originally in the first volume of Russell's *Autobiography* in 1967.

Smith's correspondence with Edward Weeks, who was his editor at *The Atlantic Monthly* and at the Atlantic Monthly Press–Little, Brown and Company, was the source of many interesting letters, which are used with the permission of Mr. Weeks and of the Humanities Center of the University of Texas at Austin, where the Weeks papers are housed. Ellen S. Dunlap, research librarian at the Center, was especially helpful there and also in directing me to letters elsewhere. The letter to Ellery Sedgwick is used with the permission of the Massachusetts Historical Society.

The letters to Edward Marsh and some of the ones to Virginia Woolf are from the Berg Collection in the New York Public Library, reprinted through the courtesy of Dr. Lola Szladits and Brian McInerney.

The large Smith collection in the Library of Congress includes many family letters from 1883 through 1938, letters to Smith from Henry James and George Santayana, some of his correspondence with Robert Bridges and Virginia Woolf, the manuscripts of several of his books and articles, and miscellaneous notes made by him between August 1939 and his death in 1946. The assistance of Charles Kelly and Gary Kohn of the Library's Manuscript Division was invaluable to me.

Sir John Pope-Hennessy sent me letters received by his mother, Dame Una Pope-Hennessy. Mrs. Igor Vinogradoff allowed me to quote from letters to her father, Philip Morrell.

Among those persons at institutions which lent me letters

(not all of which could be used) or provided me with helpful information were Michael Halls of the King's College Library at Cambridge; Colin G. Harris, the Bodleian Library at Oxford (for letters to Robert Bridges and Gilbert Murray); Sally M. Brown at the British Library; Edwin B. Bronner, the Quaker Collection at Haverford College; Lucy Fisher West, Bryn Mawr College (for letters to Carey Thomas); Dean H. Keller, Kent State University (where there is a large and varied collection of Smith papers, diaries, essays, and notebooks); Jean F. Preston, the Princeton University Library; Susan Halpert, Harvard University Library; Patricia M. Howell, of the Beinecke Rare Book and Manuscript Library of Yale University; and Saundra Taylor, curator of manuscripts at Indiana University.

The poem that Robert Bridges wrote to Smith on receiving a copy of *Trivia* is reproduced with the permission of Lord Bridges, grandson of the poet, who also allowed me to see the Bridges letters.

Leon Edel kindly read the numerous references to Henry James, and Alexander R. James, the novelist's nephew and literary heir, permitted me to reproduce a letter James wrote to Smith about a young poet, Digby Mackworth Dolben.

For the delightful letter that Gilbert Murray wrote to Smith about his Quaker heritage and for the letters from Smith to him, I owe thanks to his literary heir, Alexander Murray.

Among many others who gave me their time and shared their knowledge I should mention William Royall Tyler, holder of Edith Wharton's literary rights; Dr. Dermod Mac-Carthy, son of Desmond MacCarthy; Steele Commager, of the classics department at Columbia University; Prof. John G. Slater of the department of philosophy at the University of Toronto; Louis Barron, editorial director, Universe Books; Linda Glick Conway, managing editor, Houghton Mifflin Company; and Lady Anne Hill, who was a friend of Smith.

The Cyril Connolly quotation from which the title of the book is taken is used with the permission of Mrs. Peter Levi, Connolly's widow.

[xxxi]

Chester Kerr's personal interest in the book from its inception is much appreciated, as is the unfailing efficiency and kindness of my other editors, Katrina Kenison and Lois Randall.

To my wife, Emily, fell many tedious tasks in checking typed transcriptions against original letters and corrections; and her diligence in this was exceeded only by her help in the undertaking as a whole. My gratitude to her is great.

Editor's Note

The selections in this book were taken from about two hundred of the nearly two thousand of Smith's letters that are known to exist. They seemed to me the most entertaining, informative, and stimulating of the correspondence and best showed the originality of his mind and the quality of his writing style.

Since this is a book of selections, I have dispensed with the usual scholarly apparatus and made choices — long and short — freely from any parts of the letters without indicating omissions. In many cases the complete letters were crowded with routine matters of ordinary business and family concerns, and thus nothing of interest to us was lost in the cutting. Salutations and closings I considered unnecessary since the recipient of each letter is clearly named and the last words were the usual pleasantries. Smith's use of the terms *thee* and *thou* — especially in the early letters to members of his family — was the product of his Quaker upbringing, and added a note of warmth and affection. Obvious slips in spelling, repeated words, and slight inconsistencies in style were corrected silently, but they were few. The occasional ampersand has been expanded to *and*. The original punctuation, somewhat formal by today's standards, has been maintained. Where Smith's punctuation was illegible, I supplied the marks that seemed reasonable to me. Any words added to fill a gap in the text were set in brackets. Dates and places of writing for a number of letters have been supplied by me in brackets from postmarks or contextual evidence.

In deciphering Smith's handwriting, any editor is at Smith's mercy. Ellery Sedgwick, who was editor of *The Atlantic Monthly* for part of the time when Smith was writing for it, described to Mrs. Winthrop Chanler "the unspeakable inscrutabilities" of his manuscripts. "In one particularly intricate passage, which I pored over with a reading glass," he wrote, "I read in the first sentence 'sculptures all heads' but now my interpretation is the indubitable one 'captures all hearts.' " I have had the same experience, but I have also had the invaluable help of John Russell and Hugh Trevor-Roper in checking my transcriptions of the letters for accuracy. In a few cases where words eluded me completely, in spite of all my efforts and help from others, I inserted the word *illegible* in brackets. This had to be done in the case of some proper names, which are, of course, particularly hard to read. In a few cases I eliminated names for other reasons, mainly because they might cause unacceptable pain or because the identity added nothing to the story or comment. Smith was known for his sharp tongue, but it seems to me that his letters were singularly free of offensive or libelous matters; I have been happy to leave in certain passages in which the element of teasing is high-spirited, rather than malicious.

Smith's letters naturally raise the question of whether a man who paid so much attention to his published writing might in the more spontaneous role of correspondent fall short of the high standards he set for himself. This readers will have to decide for themselves, but I believe the letters are fresh, exciting, and in many ways equal or superior to Smith's more formal writings.

Chronology

1865	October 18, Logan Pearsall Smith born in Millville, N.J.
1868	Family moved back to Philadelphia.
1872	First trip to England.
1880	William Penn Charter School, Philadelphia.
1881–1884	Haverford College.
1884–1885	Harvard University.
1885–1886	University of Berlin.
1886–1887	Employed in New York office of family glass business.
1888	Enrolled at Oxford. Family went to live in England.
1889	Family leased Friday's Hill estate in Sussex.
1891	Graduated from Oxford. Paris. Beginning of serious efforts to become a writer.
1895	Leased High Buildings near Friday's Hill. *The Youth of Parnassus.*
1896–1899	Visited and traveled in Italy. Edited review, *The Golden Urn*, with Bernard Berenson.
1902	*Trivia* published privately.
1907	*The Life and Letters of Sir Henry Wotton.*

1909	*Songs and Sonnets.*
1912	*The English Language.* Leased Ford Place, a country house in Sussex, near Arundel.
1913	Naturalized as a British subject. Bought Big Chilling, an Elizabethan manor house at Warsash on the Hampshire coast as country place.
1914	Moved to 11 St. Leonard's Terrace, Chelsea.
1917–1918	*Trivia* published in commercial editions in America and England.
1919	*A Treasury of English Prose,* an anthology. *An Essay on Donne's Sermons,* an anthology.
1920	*Stories from the Old Testament Retold,* a pamphlet published by Virginia Woolf's Hogarth Press. *Little Essays Drawn from the Writings of George Santayana.*
1921	Returned to America for an operation at Johns Hopkins Hospital in Baltimore.
1921–1922	*More Trivia* published in England and America.
1925	*Words and Idioms,* a collection of essays.
1928	*A Treasury of English Aphorisms.*
1930	*The Golden Grove: Selections from the Sermons and Writings of Jeremy Taylor.*
1931	*Afterthoughts.*
1933	*On Reading Shakespeare.*
1933–1934	*All Trivia* (including "Last words") published in England and America.
1936	*Reperusals and Recollections,* essays.
1938–1939	*Unforgotten Years* published in England and America.
1940–1941	*Milton and His Modern Critics.*
1946	March 2, died at 11 St. Leonard's Terrace.

1949 Posthumous publications:
The Golden Shakespeare, an anthology.
A Religious Rebel: Selected Letters of Han-
nah Whitall Smith.

A Chime of Words

An American
Student Abroad

> Would Fate, we deliciously wondered, ever
> vouchsafe to us to enunciate those syllables of
> sweet magic and then win admission to those
> far-away bright circles of European culture,
> circles as heavenly in our provincial eyes as those
> circling rings seen in great Italian pictures.
>
> — *Unforgotten Years*

*Smith later referred to his year of study at the University of
Berlin as the acquiring of "some tincture of that German
learning which was considered by Americans in the 1880's as
the flower and crown of culture." He wrote, however, that he
had drawn no real profit from the experience, except for the
German he learned. His letters to his family in this winter of
1885–1886 described the student life and travel in Europe
then. He was twenty years old and the letters were those of a
very young man, filled with opinions and attitudes that would
change as he matured.*

A Tourist's Duty

Nuremberg
TO HIS SISTER MARY   October 12, 1885

We left Munich today and hated to, too. Do go there on a
wedding trip sometime — there is so much to see that I am
sure thee wouldn't get bored. We were on the go morning,

afternoon and evening. In travelling around in this way one is enabled to make a most interesting and valuable study — the budding and growth of a new moral sense, a new sense of duty; the slow rise of the tourist conscience which has the guidebook for its Bible and an indefinite Socratic "at home" for its Heaven or Hell. Woe for him who has left undone those things which Baedeker says he ought to have done, fearful is the fate which threatens him on his return home, from some scornful chorus of fellow tourists, better and stronger than he; while the anticipated bliss of proudly saying "I did it" carries many a weary tourist through what is to him a weary desert of churches and picture galleries. There is a little picture gallery at The Hague (not the big one) which Father and I did not visit though Baedeker had starred it (awful sign) and now we silently avoid people who have been in Holland, but I am sure we shall not escape. This new moral sense, like the other, is a fatal enemy to art, pictures become so many square yards to it — churches are done like one's wash, by the dozen. But enough of seriousness.

A Student's Schedule

[Berlin]
TO HIS SISTER ALYS   November 23, 1885

I will bet that I will learn more than you do this Winter — just look at my list of lectures —

> 4 hrs. a week – history of philosophy
> 4 hrs. a week – Kant's philosophy
> 4 hrs. a week – ethics
> 2 hrs. a week – introduction to philosophy
> 1 hr. a week – *neben die Pessimismus*
> 1 hr. a week – neben der Romantische
> oper der Deutschen
> 1 hr. a week – problems of Ethik
> 1 hr. a week – history of monarchy,
> democracy, etc.
> 1 hr. a week – old Vedic mythology

Besides that, I have six hours a week in German lessons, so thee sees I am not idle.

I don't have any examinations, however, so I needn't work any harder than I want. I take notes in a mixture of German and English, German when the professor talks slowly, English when he gets going faster. I had to try to find what professors I could understand before deciding on my courses, but fortunately the men I want to hear all speak *"Sehr klar und deutlich"* so I have very little trouble in understanding. Sometimes however I get a splendid long sentence almost all written out and then miss the verb and the end so that the whole thing is no good. What an awful thing it is to get an education — you have to just knit your teeth and go in and grind — according to my definition of an education, one which will enable you to pass as educated with educated people, is first of all a little science, 2ndly a thorough knowledge of English literature; 3rdly French, 4thly German, 5thly, something about music; 6thly something about art. Other things are most important, but these are the necessities, and are not to be easily obtained.

What does thee study? I really don't remember anything now that I learned in four years of college except how to play a secondrate game of whist.

I know quite a number of students here, almost all Americans, some are genuine friends, some not, but all interesting. Under strict orders from my dentist, I go to the opera two or three times a week, it is good and cheap and gives me a splendid chance to hear Wagner — so far I have heard 5 or 6 of his operas, some, like *Tannhäuser* and *Lohengrin,* two or three times. The only trouble about Wagner is that he spoils you for all other operas. One of our best Berlin singers, Lilli Lehmann, is in America now and we mourn her loss.

A Visit to Dresden

Dresden

TO HIS SISTER ALYS   December 7, 1885

Thee may think it is odd that this letter is dated from Dresden. I know that it is not the general impression that students at the Berlin University reside in Dresden, and I will confess that it is not customary. I have however come here to hear *Siegfried* as it is very well given here, and besides I wanted a change of air. Matthew Arnold is also stopping here and sits opposite us at the *table d' hôte*. He doesn't seem at all like a poet — when I got here Saturday the Baron said, "You must see the three old English boys (i.e. sports) who are staying here" and then pointed out Mr. Arnold as one of them. Thee can imagine his surprise when I told him that it was Matthew Arnold. When we made his acquaintance I can't say that first impressions were changed.

The Aims of Education

Berlin

TO HIS SISTER ALYS   January 19, [1886]

I admire thy spirit in studying and am sure it will be of inestimable worth in after life. But while one is getting an education it is well to keep in mind just what you are about — so pardon me if I air my ideas on the subject.

Firstly, an education is no more an end in itself than is climbing trees. It must be *zweckmässig* — that is, have an aim. The aims of education are two:

I, to increase our *efficiency* in the world.

II, to increase our enjoyment of the world.

I might say III, to develop and strengthen our minds, which is really an end in itself.

(A fourth incentive to study is to increase our own importance in the world — this however oughtn't to be considered.)

Having these two, or rather three, criteria we must judge every study by them and in proportion as they fill those three ends, so is their importance. Leaving out the school studies tried by this scale the college courses arrange themselves as falling in this order of importance.

   1. German and French which come under all four rules in-

creasing our efficiency, enjoyment — and importance immensely and also affording good mental training.

2. Music and art, as increasing our enjoyment immensely. I mean, of course, not to play or paint, but to appreciate both.

3. Latin which comes under III especially and to a certain extent II and IV.

4. Greek coming under III and IV.

5. Science which comes under I, II and III to a certain extent, one doesn't need much of this, as after a certain amount any more does very little good — one good stiff course of a year, say, in physics or chemistry gives us the mental training, beyond that generalizations are enough.

6. Higher mathematics, for which I have very little use — unless one enjoys them — but even then I don't think calculus would be a joy forever like the others I have mentioned.

I forgot history and philosophy — history does little beside increasing our pleasure once in a while, our *Fähigkeit* or efficiency. Philosophy comes high up — but of that, another time. One must always keep in mind that the aim of life is *to live* — not to fill our heads like buckets — the aim of a bucket is to be full, of an engine, to work — and we are engines, not buckets. Action, as Matthew Arnold says, is three-fourths of our lives; let us increase our *Fähigkeit*, live, then the remaining one-fourth is enjoyment; let us then increase our *Fähigkeit* to enjoy. *Fähigkeit* the aim of life, *Fähigkeit* of education. Here endeth the first lesson.

Life in a Pension

[Berlin]
[SALUTATION MISSING]   [Undated]

Our introduction to pension life was very agreeable — I had the pleasure of sitting by two New England types (pensions are novelists' workshops), one, a North Avenue clergyman and his wife (he a graduate of Harvard, she of Vassar). . . . He was a fine, open, frank young man, but terribly in earnest and would brush away a joke as he would a fly; his wife was like Aunt Lill, a person who would stick a pin into anyone they didn't like and say (and think) that she did it to the glory of God — but in some other ways she was very nice — they both had consciences as inflamed as they are made in New England, I guess. He, although broad, had a great idea about changing the religious tone of Harvard; he said that there was a strong movement on foot to do it among the recent graduates and directors. When I asked him how it was going to be done he was indefinite, but said for one thing that Dr. Royce[1] should be muzzled as he thought his influence was bad. I hope to goodness they won't — as soon as the directors of a college decide by a vote what is true, and then hire someone to teach this truth found by a vote of the majority, why [there] is an end to all good work. What does thee think? The others were Bostonians who quite came up to your Howells and James ideals — they were cold at first but thawed out at the received Boston rate until they grew quite friendly. The oldest daughter, who I suppose was about thirty, had evidently been out a great deal, especially in Washington, and was very bright and talked wonderfully well — only too well, for she had a very common fault with such people, she preferred saying a bright thing to a true one and made every subject tinkle, like sleigh bells, and only once in a while brought in the moral aspect as a finishing touch, her conscience was not so inflamed probably, or else she wore a poultice in society.

[1] Josiah Royce (1855–1916), American philosopher, teacher, and essayist. He was a professor of philosophy at Harvard from 1885 until his death. He held many controversial views, including a theory of the Absolute: if one admits the presence of evil in the world, it then follows that there is an absolute principle of Truth, an all-knowing Mind of Universal Thought.

The Need of Languages

TO HIS SISTER ALYS

Berlin
February 21, [1886]

Should I delay much longer to answer thy last note I am afraid I will give the impression of being a fanatical ascetic — an appearance which I am always careful to avoid. Everyone is going to Italy now, at least all the Americans here, not to be packing up for Italy is as bad as wearing full dress to break-fast — a stamp of innate vulgarity. We go in about two weeks.

For goodness sake do learn to talk German, or at least French before thee comes over here again, it is the most awkward thing not to be able to. Fortunately, I can get [by] without much trouble in German now, but my ignorance of French is a continual source of embarrassment — so I began about a month ago to take French lessons and so am a little better off now. But really we Americans are left to grow up like weeds — we ought all to have French and German nurses — but it is too late now for most of us.

We have an American dance tomorrow, which is our third, we are really a giddy community.

An Atmosphere of Young Men

Rome

TO HIS SISTER MARY   April 28, 1886

I wish I could stick my pen into the blue Italian sky and paint for thee the Sea of Marmora or the Greek seas, or the bay of Naples, a view of which from the hills is like looking into a deep-fringed gentian (that is sometimes, ordinarily one would have to put "gum shoe" in the place of "gentian," to give the effect) — for I imagine England is rather soppy at present and that a taste of Italy would be decidedly pleasant for you.

We have been really floating in an atmosphere of young men ever since we started and some of them have been real Bandersnatches. On the boat from Greece we had a most charming comedy, a Boston young man, all that that word implies and a Chicago family in millions and war paint — the Boston young man escaped to Berlin and the Chicago people descended like a whirlwind on us yesterday at this hotel. Here in Rome we had a grim, earnest Englishwoman with three daughters hunting a rich young Englishman with a timid mother. They also fortunately escaped yesterday.

I made a sentimental pilgrimage yesterday (can thee imagine

[7]

it?) with a very nice Oxford man we have met in Italy to Keats' and Shelley's graves. I really almost had an emotion, but refrained from plucking a flower.

Juliet in a Wrapper

Hotel Paoli, Florence

TO HIS FAMILY   May 21, [1886]

Verona is a picturesque old town at the base of the Tyrolese Alps and to judge by my experience, frightfully hot. I found not the spring there but full-blown summer and it is also hot here in Florence. Fortunately the houses are cool and in the morning and evening it is delightful. I think perhaps Mother would get over her dislike for churches if she were here now, for they are the coolest parts of the town, and so by going to church you not only avoid the warmth of the future but you escape that of the present, which is the most tangible of the two here now.

I saw the house of the Capulets in Verona, the court is a livery stable instead of a garden and the Juliet I saw leaning over the balcony had on a morning wrapper and frizzed hair. Even for a Romeo with a Baedeker in his hand, that was too much, so I fled.

Oxford

Smith saw Oxford for the first time when he was a small boy; he loved the old city of honey-colored stones, green lawns, and dreaming spires for the rest of his life and went back many times — to study, to visit, and to work on his books. He wrote of it with a fervor that he gave to no other place, and his letters show the pleasure of the society he found there and recall the friendships he made. He spent his life making phrases but he never found a happier one than the one describing life at Oxford as "a taste of Paradise."

Balliol College
May 14, 1888

As thee sees, I am in Balliol, but thee can't know how charming it is. The inside is as nice as the outside, and the outside couldn't be nicer. The days go very fast, and summer seems to be creeping on at a wonderful pace. I have my breakfast served in my room at about half past eight — when I don't go out for breakfast — and then I begin work about nine, sitting at my desk by my window, into which a gargoyle grins at me. About eleven I put on my gown (it is a thing not to wear the caps more than you have to) and go out and take a piece of Latin prose to my tutor. Then I come back to work and someone generally drops in and invites me to row with him or ride bicycle or play tennis in the afternoon. If it is tennis I always refuse, but otherwise I accept, and then I send my lunch to his room, or he gets his scout to send his to me, and then we lunch together, put on the appropriate costumes and spend the afternoon in the open air. We get home by five, change, have tea and then separate for two hours' work before Hall — dinner, that is. After Hall, as you come down the steps, you see the students in their gowns playing bowls on the grass in the quad, which is by this time yellowed by the slanting rays of the setting sun. Then you go, perhaps, to someone's room for coffee and mixed biscuits and then at eight you go back to your own room. In addition to this regular program I have been to about five or six lunch or breakfast parties in the last week, so thee sees that the opportunities for social intercourse are almost unlimited. I row twice a week in the racing four and mean to get trained and go in for the thing thoroughly. Yesterday five of us rowed down the Thames a few miles, fastened our boat, and spent about an hour picking flowers, which we brought back home to adorn our rooms.

* * *

Balliol College
October 20, 1889

V. W.[1] and Harold Russell[2] are living together now in lodgings and I go to dine with them sometimes to improve their
moral and general tone. I did not approve of their arrangements, as they both are rather lazy, so now I am trying to stir
up dissension between them, so that they will part. But they
both seem so good-natured that I don't think the prospects for
a quarrel are particularly bright, unless they could both man-
age to fall in love with the same girl. But even then I don't
believe Harold would care much! V. W. says he is writing a
handbook on flirtation, and is going to give a chapter to
American Leads. He says he is badly in need of a collaborator
who looks at it from the girls' point of view. Can thee suggest
— from observation of course — any good leads or trump
cards?

As to our staircase, it is rather a distinguished one. Beginning
at the top, I live in the tower. I have tried to make my room a
room from which everyone can take away an idea when he
reluctantly tears himself from my company, I have carefully
banished all debased art, and although many things are old, I
boast of having nothing bad. Now this is a very important
point, for Oxford standards of art are regrettably low. I went
the other day to see a Magdalen man I know, who has just
moved into lodgings, and found to my horror, sprawling over
his wall, a great picture of — what does thee think? Lord
Beaconsfield paying his respects to the Queen! What could be
more debased? So I turned the picture to the wall, and sat
down and talked to him seriously, and then took him to see my
tower home. He seemed very much moved, and just yesterday
he came to see me, and asked if I would come to see a picture
he had thought of buying. He conducted me to the shop, as if
he were taking me to church, or some sacred shrine, and led
me through the maze of purchasing freshmen to the picture,
his picture. It was by Rossetti, a great big woman's head — as
big as the face of a clock in a church steeple. Her finger was
on her lips — it might have been Lethe or Isis or something
of that kind, or it might have been called "Don't wake the

baby," with equal propriety. However, one felt that, whatever it was, it was something fine, so of course I told him to buy it. Surely that is progress — from Beaconsfield to Rossetti in two days!

My mantelpiece is now a model of chaste ornamentation. I have on it a majolica jar, with some peacock feathers in it, a statuette of a Greek lady in a flowing nightdress, and a few dinner invitations from men of light and learning in the university. The dinner invitations are few, not because I have not got a considerable accumulation hid away in other places, but because more than a few would spoil the chaste effect. Over my mantelpiece is the Blake. Now this just shows how low the standard of culture is in Oxford — I assure you that the Blake has been more than once openly scoffed at by people from whom, on account of their station and education, one ought to expect far different things. However they have to yield, although unwillingly, to its fascination. One man on our staircase made his wrists quite red and sore by trying to get his hands like Adam's, and another man has bruised his forehead in an unsuccessful attempt to stand on his head in Eve's original way. I think such gestures and postures must be only possible under strong emotional stress of some kind.

Willie Peel has a good stock of debased art, so before he came up I went to his lodgings and pasted on his things strips of paper with "Debased Art" written legibly in red ink. He however defends his things, on two pleas. (i) They are not debased, and I know nothing about it. (ii) Although debased they are of interest historically. They mark progress, and are landmarks of the past, and Carlyle says that all the Past is holy. But I tell him that things can't be said to mark progress unless there is the Before as well as the Behind. Besides his own things, he has a great many plush and terra-cotta ornaments that belong to his landlady, and he is afraid to remove them for fear of hurting her feelings.

[1] Ralph Vaughan Williams (1872–1958), one of the most famous of modern British composers.
[2] Harold Russell (1868–1926). Son of Lord Arthur Russell. Barrister-at-Law. Recorder of Bedford, 1912.

Benjamin Jowett

The most famous scholar at Oxford in Smith's time was Benjamin Jowett (1817–1893), master of Balliol and Regius Professor of Greek literature. He spent his entire adult life at Oxford and became one of its legendary figures.

He was seventy-three when Smith met him. He sometimes invited students to his cottage in the Malvern hills and it was there that Smith wrote the next two letters.

Ashfield House, West Malvern

TO HIS MOTHER   January 3, 1890

I arrived here successfully yesterday after a pleasant journey. It is high up, almost at the top of the Malvern hills, and we ought to have a fine view, but at present it consists of fog.

The Master seems cheerful, but as usual he is somewhat difficult in conversation. You ask him some question and the answer he gives seems to be not what he thinks but what he thinks will be good for you to hear. However, if you insist on it, he will give his real opinion, and then he is always interesting.

There are two other scholars of Balliol here, of that kind whose learning is so extremely profound that they find it quite impossible to express it in conversation.

* * *

TO HIS MOTHER   January 1890

The Master is very charming, but does not talk as much as one could wish, when one thinks of what he has been through. He came up to Oxford 50 years ago and has been there ever since. Some of his stories are good however — about Lord Egremont, who lived at Petworth, and in whose day the Evangelical Revival took place. He used to say "In my youth nobody was religious; now everybody is religious, and they are both wrong." That is English common sense for you. He also told us about a high church man at Oxford — a very learned man — who would not go out at night because he had

[12]

read in the Fathers that devils went about at night. He afterwards, the Master said, joined the Catholic Church.

Romance

London
April 24, 1890
TO HIS SISTER ALYS

We had a most delightful time at Torquay and I enjoyed the quiet and seclusion. It is so delightful to live with regularity. I sometimes think I should like to have my insides taken out and machinery put in. To have long cool mornings for work and plenty of exercise in the afternoon and to feel when you go to bed that you have advanced a little, have gone a little forward — that is the real and most lasting pleasure. Other things wear brighter colors but this lasts. One must prepare to be lonely, perhaps, and to give up some of the richer joys.

Since I have been at Oxford the choking cares of this world have kept me in a gasping condition, and I have not been in a mood to finish this. Delightful Oxford — to be in its streets again and to hear its talk — it does exhilarate. Hobhouse also has been seized with a longing for the domestic joys and has plighted his troth to a maiden from the North. They do not agree much about fundamentals. As someone said to me today, "A man who marries before he is 30 is a fool, but he who marries before 25 is a knave." To me such love matches contain but little harm. What women these Oxford men marry! It is stupid, pathetic — all sorts of things. Except for Mrs. Smith there is hardly a woman in Oxford — only wives. Perhaps they were so originally; perhaps they have degenerated.

Paying Your Debts

13 Museum Terrace, Oxford
[Undated]
TO HIS SISTER MARY

This term has been different to anything before. I am what is called a "fourth year man," that is I am in the class of oldest undergraduates and instead of sitting at the feet of others,

others come to study me. One thing Oxford does, it socializes one, teaches you to try at least to pay back your debts to society. In Oxford that means to hand on to the younger generation the truths, truisms, platitudes and paradoxes received from those who went before you.

My work is very interesting and teaches me to grapple with problems of thought.

On Reading
and Writing

People say that life is the thing, but I prefer
reading.

— Afterthoughts

*Smith devoted most of his life to reading and writing. The
constant reading included the widest possible range of books,
old and new, and the letters throughout this collection are
filled with references to them. He was no less interested in
writing: he called it "looking for things you really see and feel
and then describing them in the most beautiful and appropriate words." The letters in this section are mainly his
thoughts on how that could be done.*

How to Write a Good Letter

New York

TO HIS SISTER MARY   December 5, 1886

My monthly epistle is due today. . . . Every letter should be
divided, I think, into three parts: first, gossip, which you owe
it to your correspondent to write; 2ndly, personal news, which
your correspondent owes to you to read; and 3rdly, generalizations on the universe as a whole — or the particular part in
which you happen to live.

Long and Short Sentences

Friday's Hill, Haslemere

TO HIS SISTER MARY   November 2, 1892

A series of short sentences, laid down one after the other, gets rather monotonous and jerky. One should try and get a periodic style, I think; long sentences, with qualifications in them, tangling and untangling themselves (as Stevenson puts it) like knots of string, interspersed now and then with one or more quite short ones, and all bound up with paragraphs with some unity of meaning form a texture of style that both rests and interests the eye and silent ear with which one reads. Of course this is a matter for the temperament of the writer.

Morals

Venice

TO HIS MOTHER   October 23, 1895

I *do* begin to feel middle-aged and I wish I had done more. But thee mustn't feel that our generation has no sense of duty, and no desire to accomplish good things and "hasten the Coming" as the Bible says; it is only that we think a great many things good and important, and when we talk against virtue and goodness it is only against a narrow and negative formulation of them which leaves out beauty and enjoyment and the realization of the best parts of our nature. Now I scoff at a moral purpose in a novel, but it is only because I think that it is more important for literature to give us a true and poignant picture of how people act and feel, or else make people in love with the beauty of life. So, if I can influence my generation to look out for the things they really see and feel and then describe these sights and feelings in the most beautiful and appropriate words, I shall feel that I am doing quite as much, or more, good than I could do in any other way. Of course, I know these things don't seem so important, but our duty, as someone has said, is to polish and make bright, each of us, some one corner or spot of the world.

A Writer's Beginnings

*Smith reflected on what he had learned about writing in reply
to a question asked him in 1924 when he was fifty-eight years
old and in the middle of his career. The questioner was a
seventeen-year-old American, Dwight Macdonald, who later
had a successful career of his own as an essayist and critic and
polemicist. He died in 1982.*

11 St. Leonard's Terrace

TO DWIGHT MACDONALD   March 25, 1924

I am naturally flattered by the kind things that you say about
my little book *Trivia* — flattered too that you should wish to
imitate that way of writing, which I think you have done with
extraordinary charm and success. I have always thought that
the form of *Trivia*, prose Minims, or whatever one may call
them, is happily fitted to catch and reflect the moods of modern
and self-conscious people; and your excerpts confirm me in
this opinion, giving one as they do a lively and delightful
glimpse into your thoughts and life . . . I hope you will go on
in this vein — the amused observation of one's own self is a
veritable gold mine whose surface has hardly yet been
scratched.

You ask me about my own writing — when I began, and
whether I found it difficult. I began it as an American boy;
when, I suppose, I was about your age I made up my mind
to be a writer of good prose; to master, if possible, that beautiful instrument. I found it extremely difficult, for I don't think
I had any natural gift for writing. But the art of prose, unlike
that of poetry, is one that can be learnt, if one has the determination to learn it — that, rather than any early facility, is
the surest promise of success. I pegged away at it for many
years, studying the best writers, trying to imitate them, as-
siduously collecting in pocket notebooks words and phrases,
and the little thoughts that float into one's mind at odd moments (these mostly-rejected thoughts are really the golden
material of good writing); and at last I found what I wanted
to do — my "little note," as it were, and the little form in
which to embody what I most intimately felt.

This is a path that anyone who wishes can follow, for nothing can really stop a fixed determination; but one must love it for itself, and not for the rewards it brings, although these rewards are in the end certain and delightful. There are of course many lions (and many lionesses) in the path; there is self depreciation, and there is the immense and universal conspiracy of family, friends and the whole world to stop one — a conspiracy so potent in America that I found it necessary to escape from that country and take refuge at Oxford and in England, where one is left free to cultivate one's little talent without interference. But the worst lion in the path is one that I happily escaped — the lion of an early and premature success, which makes one satisfied with one's facile and acceptable writing, and keeps one back from the lonely and difficult path which alone leads to excellence.

If you mean to be a writer, I should like to suggest, if I may give you advice, that, without losing sight of your ultimate goal, you should devote as much of your youth as you can to obtaining a good foundation in the classics — without some knowledge of Greek and Latin one cannot be a really educated person. If you miss getting this knowledge in your youth, you will bitterly regret it all your life. Practice writing by all means, but give your main thoughts to getting a thorough knowledge of the ancient and modern classics. I am afraid I have a low opinion of American education and its results, and I often bless the happy star that led me from Harvard to Oxford.

Among modern writers the ones I find most useful, and who have most helped me are Montaigne and Charles Lamb and Flaubert and Pater. Montaigne taught me to look into my own mind; Pater and Lamb gave me an ideal of what good English prose should be, and Flaubert's letters were a kind of Bible, which preached to me the religion of art, and the contempt of the rewards and joys and successes of ordinary existence. All this was no doubt somewhat precious and perhaps affected, but to be so is, perhaps, in an age of universal vulgarity and low standards, a necessary attitude for one who is serious in his love of quality, and who has set his heart upon attaining it — or at least of dying in its pursuit.

All this will sound to you perhaps fantastic, foolish and old-fashioned. I generally feel myself in the presence of the younger generation an extinct kind of mammal, mumbling my old and out-of-date idealisms in an obsolete kind of language which no one now understands or cares to listen to.

With regard to your other enquiries I am all in favor of the split-infinitive in its proper place. Let me recommend to you an excellent essay in the Society for Pure English, Tract No. 15, *The Split Infinitive*, which any book-seller can get for you from the Oxford University Press. Tract No. 12 in the same series on *English Idioms* (written by me) might also interest you — a feeling for idiom, and the right use of it, is most important for anyone wishing to write good English. If that remains your wish, write to me later on, and I will be glad to help you if I can.

The Ideal in Literature

The Criterion *magazine for July 1924 contained an article by Virginia Woolf on "Character in Fiction," in which she contrasted three novelists she called Edwardians — John Galsworthy, Arnold Bennett, and H. G. Wells — with several newer writers — E. M. Forster, D. H. Lawrence, Lytton Strachey, James Joyce, and T. S. Eliot. To make her point, Mrs. Woolf considered the potential drama in the life of a woman she called Mrs. Brown, whom she had observed in a train, and how her story would have been told — or not told — by the Edwardian novelists, who placed emphasis on social conditions rather than on character. They would have lost Mrs. Brown, she wrote, because they would not have really looked at her, but at the facts of the surface world around her. Thus, they would have failed to express character — and that is what the novel as a form had evolved to do.*

Big Chilling, Hampshire
July 15, 1924

I feel it "borne in upon me" as the Quakers say, to make a few remarks — if I may be allowed to do so — on your paper in the *Criterion,* which I have just read — as I read everything you write — with joy and envy, since it becomes more and more obvious that your pen beats all our pens. It seems to me that you have really given yourself the answer to the question that you put in this paper — you *have* caught your Mrs. Brown — caught her triumphantly and neatly, made her a living reality to us and, as it were, a part of our own experience. What more can we want? People only exist for us in our thoughts about them, our reflections, our observations, our experiences of them, our reactions to them, our surmises about them. They float like slow, strange fish in the pools or aquarian tanks of our imaginations. That is their reality; why attempt to construct another hypothetical or bogus reality for them; or, when you have caught your Mrs. Brown, drop the poor lady to rush after a conventional image of her?

Isn't the whole tendency of the time, and the great interest of it, the discovery and exploration of our consciousness, this getting closer to the actual texture of life and experience; this seeing things as they exist for us, floating in the stream of our own consciousness, and not gasping or flopping about on a dry land, and in an empty atmosphere, of which we have no knowledge? Just as the form of the objective drama has become impossible for us as a form in which to embody our experience, so won't the objective novel (which is born of the drama) also become impossible, with its attempt to create characters with a dramatic existence abstracted from our thoughts about them? It is this way of seeing people, not as we think they actually are, but as they are seen in the author's mind (as in Proust) or in the mirrors of each other's minds (as in Henry James) which seems to me the interesting modern discovery and I think this is a convention and a form which is capable of an immense and fruitful application.

But the interest and importance of this discovery doesn't at all make me feel that we are, as you say you believe (but perhaps this is only your fun), "trembling on the verge of one of the great ages of English literature." Great ages of art seem to me, from my reading of history, to proceed from other causes than new discoveries of reality, though these discoveries no doubt help in the general result, when the other conditions are favorable, and the other stars combine in a happy conjunction. Perfection of form, accomplishment, beauty, are occasional and it would seem — almost accidental visitants — transitory gleams on the stream of existence; and we know very little of what makes them appear or disappear. I think it is more a question of form and of technique than of material and the happiest prognostic to my mind of a dawn in any art is an interest in the technical side of that art and experiments in its special vehicle. The vehicle of literature is words, their meanings, their overtones and echoes and the effects which can be produced by the juxtapositions of their wonder-working sounds and it seems to me that the great periods of literature have always been preceded by — or accompanied by — a great interest in words and excitement about them — periods of enthusiasm and experiments in language. As I see not the slightest sign of such interest at present, I cannot feel hopeful about the future of literature — in our times, at least. The crepuscle or twilight which seems to you a dawn looks to me uncommonly like an approaching and rapidly descending night of literature. And, after all, why should we weep over the sunset when we know that if the sun never set, it would never rise again? Fine things are all the finer for being a while forgotten; literary forms, and languages themselves, become exhausted, and need to be fallow for a time, and when the Spring comes they will germinate and spring up in a fashion all the more lively for the restful winter they have been through.

But this is hardly an evangel to send to the address of a contemporary publisher! It is my interest in your article which has led me into this long disquisition which I have written with a freer pen, since I know my ideas are so out of fashion that no one ever listens to them — like the sole survivor of a race of extinct mammals, I go on mumbling my old idealisms in a tongue which has long since been forgotten.

[21]

On the Art of Writing

There are many letters in this collection to Kenneth Clark, later Lord Clark of Saltwood, a leading figure in the art world. Clark was 23, a disciple of Berenson's, and obviously headed for a splendid career when he met Smith at I Tatti in 1926. They became friends at once and Smith agreed to teach him to write, but said it was clear that the younger man needed no teaching. Clark was at one time director of the National Gallery in London, then chairman of the Arts Council of Great Britain, and he achieved worldwide success with a famous television series called Civilisation. *In 1927 he married Jane Martin and many of Smith's letters are addressed to her. Clark died in 1983.*

I Tatti

TO KENNETH CLARK   1926

Now I am getting to work on those "Letters on the Art of Writing" that we spoke of. I find it an admirable plan (for me at least) to have someone to crank up my poor old talents; Walter Raleigh[1] made me do Donne's sermons and most of *Words and Idioms* was written for our poet.[2] You see at least that you are in good company. My self-starter seems badly out of order. The truth is, that I got on so long — and not at all unhappily — without appreciation, that such success as I have had in recent years has come so late that I have never really believed in it. I have got out of the habit of thinking that people read my books, though I can't help knowing that they buy them — the gold seems to me like fairy gold, and I regard it as no more than a pleasant mirage, those shining pools which might promise to slake my natural thirst for appreciation. But to write with the certainty of at least one genuine reader will make a great difference and I think these letters will go on very well.

[1] Sir Walter Raleigh (1861–1922) was professor of English literature at Oxford from 1904 and was regarded by his contemporaries as a major authority on the subject.
[2] Robert Bridges, who is introduced later in the section on Smith's friends.

I was much pleased to get your letter; I don't want to force
an unwelcome correspondence on you, but I shall always be
glad to hear from you, and will answer with due promptness.
Only the notion of my teaching you to write seems more and
more absurd, since you write so well already. However, I
should like to keep up the farce, since this pretense provides
me with the thing that is most welcome to authors, especially
as they grow older — a loose, free form, a large, capacious
basket in which they can put all the goods they happen to
have on hand. I have been throwing the ink about with
great vigor and have already written seven more letters. As,
however, I am rushing ahead while the mood is on me, I
haven't stopped to give any of them a more polished shape;
this I can do later when the divine afflatus leaves me; and
anyhow, as what I have written is mostly retrospection,
"books that have helped me," etc., and general ideas on
literature, its interest will not be so great to you as the more
practical and "prosy" letters I hope to write later. I am much
enjoying this bout of writing; prose seems to pour from me
as from a broached beer barrel; my ideas seem new, amusing,
brilliant and original to myself. But their very fluency makes
me uneasy — can it be that the *zeitgeist* is making me its
speaking tube and bellowing through me the ideas which the
man in the street is thinking, or about to think?

Thomas Hardy

I Tatti, Florence

TO KENNETH CLARK   Early in 1926

This Hardy business[1] is becoming as serious for me as it is
for you . . . Bob Trevelyan, who is staying here, keeps preaching a modified Hardyism at me on the line that an artist with
a harsh voice and bad technique can sometimes get effects of
great value out of his defects themselves — like Beethoven,
he says, but I don't know enough about Beethoven to refute
him there. Then, too, that viper Reason, keeps hissing at me
that it is folly to let one's prejudices blind one to beauty, in a

world where there is not too much beauty. I hate that viper, though I have often in the past profited by its whisper. Still, I stand firm, though again I wonder whether my firmness is anything more than the will of the old enemy, who, in his rage for change, wishes to throw down Hardy and put someone else upon his pedestal.

¹ Smith had referred to Thomas Hardy as "the famous master of clumsy phrases and undistinguished diction."

Travel Writing
TO HIS SISTER MARY   March 26, 1930

I have now gone through thy manuscript¹ and am sending thee herewith some verbal criticisms, nothing of much importance but a sort of hair-combing of the text.

On the whole I like the book very much and think it a really fine book of travel, vivid and alive and full of interest and thought, but I think it might be and ought to be much better and that with a certain amount of trouble thee could improve it immensely.

What makes a book of travel interesting is not facts and information, but the large ideas they illustrate, and the facts should come in as illustrations of general ideas — not as mere statements of what has happened or what the traveller saw. This is thy method in the later chapters, which are luminous with ideas, but there is to my mind too much mere information in the earlier ones. The French mandate, for instance, the history of Lady Hester Stanhope, of Tyre and Sidon . . . Thy geographical account of Palestine is, I think, too detailed. All this is too guidebooky, especially as the subjects are so well known.

¹ Mary Berenson wrote three books. The one referred to here was *A Modern Pilgrimage* and was about Palestine, published by Appleton in New York in 1930. *Across the Mediterranean*, published in Italy by Giachetti at Prato in 1935, was an account of a journey to Tunisia and Algeria. Her next book, *A Vicarious Trip to the Barbary Coast*, was compiled from letters sent back to her from her husband and members of a party who made the trip. There were interpolations by her on Libya. It was published by Constable in London in 1938.

On Perfection

TO HIS SISTER MARY April 18, 1930

Don't let them hurry thee too much about the book — the date of publication really doesn't matter, and there is no pleasure like that of rewriting, and polishing one's phrases — I could have told thee that long ago.

> "The indefatigable pursuit of unattainable perfection, though it consists in nothing more than pounding an old piano, is what alone can give a meaning to life on this sad and unavailing star."

That's my latest and wisest aphorism.[1]

[1] This appeared later in *Afterthoughts*.

Beautiful Phrases

TO ROBERT GATHORNE-HARDY April 1, 1930

I am nourishing by the way rather a grievance against you — I felt the other day — or was I wrong? — that you didn't appreciate the sentence that I read you about the Mediterranean waters, "The radiance streaming towards him from the luminous and unfading azure at his feet."[1]

But you are young, so I forgive you, and hope that when you are older you will realize that a beautiful phrase is the most important thing in the world — that nothing else really matters.

[1] From C. K. Scott Moncrieff's translation of Proust.

On Publishing Books

11 St. Leonard's Terrace

TO HIS SISTER MARY November 27, 1933

I have a whole collection of essays which I certainly mean to reprint sometime, and now and then I take them out and tinker at them. But I am in no hurry. I don't much like publishing books — the misprints will creep in and the floods of letters I get from strangers I find a bore, and I don't much

[25]

care for publicity. To shine alone in the limelight — or with a few choice spirits — would be pleasant, but now-a-days one finds oneself in such degrading company! And to be praised by third-rate journalists is a kind of ignominy — the slush I get from America about my *Shakespeare* really turns my stomach. Even if my pearls are false and the grunts of the genuine swine are also genuine, the whole proceeding has something about it which doesn't seem to me "quite nice." However, this is rather priggish, and I certainly like getting money from my books, if nothing else.

* * *

TO KENNETH CLARK

11 St. Leonard's Terrace
January 6, 1935

I have been very well and happy this autumn — too happy, I fear, to be really well, as I am suffering from — and enjoying — an attack of what is called euphoria, a kind of exaltation brought on I think by having a lot of teeth extracted. This shows itself in the usual forms, intense enjoyment of everything, sense of fun, love of practical jokes and also (a common symptom — William James used to have attacks of it, and also Landor) the belief that I am endowed with an infallible judgment about pictures so I go out and quite often buy masterpieces for almost nothing on the King's Road. Another form of this delicious megalomania is the feeling that I am writing pages and pages of wonderful prose. I am fattening out my article on Shakespeare (written in my last attack of euphoria) with beautiful new pages and splash about the purple ink in my elderly inkpot with a furore of delight. It's all great fun even though it may lead me into an asylum — it will have been worth it.

What Is Countenance?

Sir Edward Marsh (1872–1953) was a man of many activities in the social, political, and literary London of his time. He was at one time secretary to Winston Churchill. He was something of a literary dictator, having edited the

Georgian Poetry *anthologies (five volumes published between 1912 and 1922). Also he translated the fables of La Fontaine (1931) and wrote a memoir of his friend Rupert Brooke. At the time of this letter he had just published his reminiscences,* A Number of People.

I am enjoying my convalescence thoroughly and reading Jane Austen for the hundredth time. Here is a nice point in her vocabulary which I should like to submit to your consideration. What exactly does she mean by "countenance"? Henry Crawford [in *Mansfield Park*] had so much of it that the Bertram young women revised their first opinion, and would not allow that he was plain. It could be acquired. Both Sir Thomas Bertram and Harry Crawford noticed Fanny Price had acquired it in the six weeks Sir Thomas had been away. It wasn't gravity, as Mrs. Gardiner [in *Pride and Prejudice*] insists to Elizabeth Bennet that Wickham possessed more "countenance" than Darcy. What was it exactly then? Who do you think possesses it today? Lady Desborough[1], I should say, and Lady Hamilton[2]; old Countess Bencke[3] was a splendid example. Lady Horner[4] has it almost to excess, as she has consequence also, which a lady of consequence among my neighbors says is called "putting on airs" by servants.

"Countenance" is rare among men, I should say, now-a-days — Maurice Baring[5] has it, and Asquith[6] had it, but who else?

[1] Lady Desborough was a leading Edwardian hostess in London.
[2] Lady Hamilton, another prominent hostess, was seen by her friends as a fusion of fashion and intellect.
[3] Countess Benckendorff was the wife of the last Czarist Russian ambassador to England.
[4] Lady Horner had a literary salon in London and was, in Edward Marsh's opinion, "the wisest of women."
[5] Maurice Baring (1874–1945), British novelist and autobiographer.
[6] Herbert Henry Asquith (1852–1928), British statesman and prime minister from 1908 to 1916.

* * *

With all due respect, I don't think that you have really grasped
the full meaning of "countenance," as Jane Austen used it. I
have received (indirectly) this note from G. M. Young[1] which
seems to me to get nearer the truth:

"Johnson gives as one definition of countenance, 'Confi-
dence of mien, assurance of aspect.'"

G. M. Y. points out that this is the sense you get in the
phrases "out of countenance" "in good countenance." This,
he says, "exactly suits Fanny [Price, in *Mansfield Park*] and
the others too because it can easily be exaggerated into bold-
ness or over-boldness as with Wickham and Crawford while
Darcy [in *Pride and Prejudice*] and Knightley [in *Emma*]
seem to have an inner reserve of modesty or shyness." I think
this good, but how could one have applied it to Lady Wigram
who, as you say, had it in the supreme degree? . . .

[1] George Malcolm Young (1882–1959), a distinguished historian.

Jane Austen as Henry James

*Robert William Chapman, an Oxford scholar and secretary
of the Clarendon Press of the University, brought out the
standard edition of the works of Jane Austen, beginning in
1923. Edward Marsh criticized the edition in the* London
Mercury, *and the subsequent exchange of letters between
him and Chapman is referred to in the next letter.*

11 St. Leonard's Terrace

The sentence where Jane Austen imitates Henry James is
towards the beginning of Chapter XI of *Emma*:

The bustle and joy of such an arrival, the many to be talked
to, welcomed, encouraged, and variously dispersed and dis-
posed of, produced a noise and confusion which his nerves
could not have borne under any other cause, nor have en-

dured much longer even for this; but the ways of Hartfield and the feelings of her father were so respected by Mrs. John Knightley, that in spite of maternal solicitude for the immediate enjoyment of her little ones, and for their having instantly all the liberty and attendance, all the eating and drinking, and sleeping and playing, which they could possibly wish for, without the smallest delay, the children were never allowed to be long a disturbance to him, either in themselves or in any restless attendance on them.

I owe you a grudge, by the way, since you are after Chapman with a knife, he is making a whipping boy of me, for he is going over the proofs of a Society for Pure English paper I have written on "Romantic Words" with a malignant microscope for phrases and references and quotations. Or perhaps it is his revenge for the mistake I found on Page 413 of his *Pride and Prejudice*

"Mrs. Annesley pp 226" (for pp 127)

Chapman being a man like Shelley's Miss Hitchens "of desperate views and dreadful passions, but of cool and considering revenge." So, look out!

The Meaning of Rhetoric

Robert Calverley Trevelyan (1872–1951) was a close friend of Smith's for many years and a correspondent to whom he wrote long and thoughtful letters. Trevelyan was a member of a family of famous British historians, son of Sir George Trevelyan and brother of George Macaulay Trevelyan. He himself wrote poetry, plays, and essays. One friend referred to "the disorderly riches of his mind which was a junk shop of wisdom and learning," and Bertrand Russell said he was "the most bookish person I ever knew." Smith particularly enjoyed his company, and there are many references to him throughout these letters.

Thanks for the enchanting book with its lovely title [*Wind-falls*]. It is the kind of book I love most, mellow and mature, and full of wit and fine phrases. I didn't know you could write such charming prose! The autobiographical passages pleased me especially, and I suggest, for the blank book, a more complete account of your adventures among books and persons.

Being a word-wrangler, I want to quarrel with you about some of your nouns and adjectives:

Rhetoric: You don't define what you mean by rhetoric. To me, as to others, it implies an audience to be persuaded to something. Milton, as I remember, says in his letter to Hartlib that the art of rhetoric is the art of persuasion. The poet, in my opinion, expressed himself, the orator speaks to others. I have written on this in my essay on Jeremy Taylor (reprinted in my volume *Reperusals* pp. 209–210), where, by the way, you will find Henry James' use of long-tailed similes, as well as Jeremy Taylor's, in English prose (p. 297).

Lyrical: With the modern narrowing and deepening of the word's meaning (lyrics like those of Catullus, Shelley and Goethe) it is now almost an anachronism to speak (as you do) of Pindar as a lyric poet, though when Young (of the *Night Thoughts*)[1] wrote in the Eighteenth century an essay on lyric poetry he was quite right to make Pindar's odes his principal subject.

Your suggestion of *Kindness* for charity or love I think admirable. It's an old usage — the Oxford dictionary finds it in the Thirteenth century, and quotes Macbeth's "milk of human kindness" and Samuel Smiles' "kindness does not consist in gifts, but in gentleness and generosity of spirit." Its usage in place of "love" is now rare, the dictionary says. I will do what I can to promote it. Will you in turn help me to introduce into English the fine French word *bougresse*? Flaubert (that master of words) when he wrote from Egypt called the pyramids *ces vieilles bougresses*. It would be a useful word to describe . . . and suchlike ancient females. For their male counterparts I suggest *bougre*. Cyril [Connolly] has

printed the words in *Horizon* — or more decently, *Pagod,*
used by Pope —

> *See thronging Millions to the Pagod run,*
> *And offer Country, Parent, Wife or Son.*

¹ *Night Thoughts on Life, Death and Immortality* by Edward Young (1683–1765), a poem written in blank verse in nine books defending Christian orthodoxy against free thinkers and libertines.

In the Beginning Was the Word . . .

Gilbert Murray (1866–1957), professor of Greek at Oxford and a classical scholar and translator of Greek dramas, was a man Smith admired and in whose company he found much pleasure. Murray was also a public figure, and at the time of this letter was chairman of the League of Nations Union.

TO GILBERT MURRAY　　　　　　November 9, 1944

I imagine that you and the other Leaguers may now be giving your consideration to the naming of that new Phoenix which we all hope will replace the League of Nations. Perhaps you have already found a fitting appellation; if not, I should like to offer a few considerations. You are as well aware as I am that every form of speech follows laws of its own and is quite beyond the control of any individual or any group of reformers. They are but bubbles on a stream whose torrent they can't dam or divert by any "basic" proposals for drastic changes in spelling, syntax, or grammar.

"Behold now Behemoth!" This admonition echoes in my ears when I sit on the banks of the great sea of human speech. "Canst thou draw out Leviathan with a hook?" "Canst thou lead by the nose the hippopotamus or great water-horse of that mighty stream?" Can Mrs. Partington of Sidmouth fight against the Atlantic Ocean? Curiously enough the answer to these queries is in the affirmative. It *is* given, to certain favored beings, to influence and augment the resources of language. But not all are worthy of their opportunities: scientists, for example, are of all men the least fitted

for word-creation. Instead of choosing a convenient and un-
occupied sound like *gas* they reconstruct out of old bones and
fossils immense skeletons of nomenclature, and the notion
never seems to occur to them that what is needed for a new
discovery or invention is not a word containing its own explanation, but a brief convenient label. One of the most emi-
nent and prolific of these abortionists once told me that his
method of creating his long explanatory combinations was to
take a Greek dictionary with him into his bath, and dig from
it the right Greek roots to define his meaning to other scientists. When I asked him whether these other scientists could
read Greek — "Not one of them," he cheerfully replied, "can
read a word of it, any more than I can."

Whether frightened by these monstrosities, or terrified by
the teeth-gnashing on the bank, *The Times,* that monster of
the river torrent, has become the victim of a still more dreadful tendency — "alphabetization," or the use of initials for
miscreating words. This linguistic transgression was invented,
as far as I can learn, by the Roman pedant, Serenus Sam-
monicus, who is chiefly remembered for a letter of his, preserved by Macrobius, on the honors rendered at banquets to
that great river fish, the sturgeon. This pedant was murdered
at a fish-banquet by order of the Emperor Caracalla, but un-
luckily not before he had invented, by combining the initial
letters ABRA (being the names of the holy AB, BEN,
RUACH and ACADOSH) the art of Abracadabra writing.
Would that Caracalla had killed Serenus before this feast,
for to me at least (though my contemporaries seem to revel
in it) this O.K. way of writing isn't O.K. in the least. The
B.B.C. I know; but when I read in the *New Statesman* that
"Critic" has been unjustly accused of saying that the E.L.A.M.
and the E.L.A.S. are never mentioned by the B.B.C., although
they were more active than the E.K.K.A., this conflict is really
all Greek to me. The older N.C.O., and the newer A.R.P.
and R.A.F. I understand, but what are the M.O.T., the
P.B.I., the S.E.A.C., the M.I.N. of France and the I.C.O.
of my native country? I haven't the slightest notion; and this
way of abracadabracally creating words seems to my mind

likely to produce the worst linguistic disaster since the catastrophe of Babel.

Is all lost then? Shall the races of the earth return again to the state of things after Babel, when no man could understand the speech of his neighbors? It isn't quite so bad as that. Many of these abracadabras have a wide currency and will also sometimes coalesce by chance into a word which can be easily pronounced. We see WREN and ENSA and SHAEF and WAAC; and even UNRRA is now becoming a word. The consideration of UNRRA has led me to entertain a notion which I dare not suddenly produce, as it would probably arouse in you (as it would in me, in similar circumstances) that fury and nausea which Coleridge called "miso-neism" — that automatic reaction to any proposed linguistic innovation, good or bad. Therefore, to delay a moment the proffering to your lips of this execrable cup, and to soften you, as they say now, for the bomb whose explosion I have been preparing, I will mention three facts which I think worth pondering.

(i) Any new word will always, or almost always, lack the resonance of those old names which have been enriched by the heritage and echoes of history. Words like "Athens," or "Rome," or a poet's name like "Keats" (which might have been "Thens" or "Bome" or "Beets") owe their music to the associations which Time can, and may, bestow on any convenient collocation of vowels and consonants.

(ii) The New Jerusalem won't and can't find its home on the site of Washington or London, or even, I fear, that of Geneva; and the constitution on which it will be founded will almost certainly be based on the phrase "United Nations."

(iii) I tried to think at first that the two initials U and N might coalesce in the word we need; but such a coalescence would result in the word "UN" which, pronounced (as it should be) YOON, would sound as weighty to the ear as, say, LEAGUE; yet to the eye it would look too brief and unimportant for the weight of the meaning it would have to bear. In fact the Genus of the language wouldn't touch it.

But why not, I then asked myself, steal a leaf from the

book of Dictators and form a "portmanteau" word like *Cheka*, *Nazi*, and *Gestapo*, out of deliberately chosen letters, arranged to form a word which the world might be forced to swallow? Why not baptize the new institution the "United Nations Association of Total Effort," and thus create the word UNATE to unite and league all the nations of the world together?

So here the cat is out of the bag and I lift the execrable cup to your lips at last. Let me urge in its favor the noble ancestry and Indo-Germanic pedigree of both the syllables in this combination. A noble ancestry, though not a necessity, is no disadvantage to a newborn word. Also UNATE can be used both as a noun and as a verb, and an adjective UNATIVE can be formed from it, and echoes and associations from the "United States" of America, and from the adjectives "uniform" and "unanimous" would help give dignity to the term.

In the Beginning was the Word, and to those who take a linguistic rather than a theological or Marxist view of history, the nations of the world have made war on each other in vain wars of words. Those Sons of Darkness, the would-be Dominators of the World, have proved in some way more worldly-wise than the Sons of Light. Though Julius Caesar confessed that with all his power he wasn't able to add one word to the language, his modern imitators have learned the trick. We have often been told that the Few steal power from the Many because they are more alert and more wholeheartedly devoted to their aims. Our mild perfectionists and vegetarian Peace-Leaguers won't like my word UNATE any more than I like it myself, but I am equally certain that they won't take the trouble to find or invent — how I wish to Heaven they would — a more animating motto for our banners before we are led forth like sheep led by sheep to the slaughter, all bleating S.O.S.

Coining New Words

Peter Quennell (1905–   ), critic and biographer, was joint editor of History Today *until 1979.*

TO PETER QUENNELL   July 9, 1943

Nothing interests me more than the coining of new words, and if I could add one to the currency of language I should die happy. I tried to revive the old borrowing *malease* once, for the French and unassimilated *malaise*; it had a run in the *Times Literary Supplement* for a while, but now has faded again. Two people I have known have added words to the vocabulary of Europe — Austin Harrison with *suffragette* and Roger Fry[1] with *Post-Impressionist*. Bad formations, but indispensable in their time.

I hope you can prove that *sentimental* was coined by Sterne — he certainly added it to the European vocabulary.

[1] Roger Fry (1866–1934), painter and critic, and a member of the Bloomsbury group. A supporter of radical artistic innovations in the first two decades of this century, he helped shape the artistic taste of modern England. He was a close friend of Smith's, exchanged many letters with him (they have not been located), and painted Smith's portrait in 1922.

TO EDWARD MARSH   April 11, 1931

The S.P.E.[1] has not pronounced on fête — the difficulty of removing the accent and the pronunciation — still, on the whole I should remove it, as we certainly need the word, and it will never be at home with that foreign crown.

There is nothing I love more than quibbling about words, but there are so few people to quibble with. You are almost the only one.

"So eager" can be defended I think as the mere intensive without comparative force — for example Keats' line in *Lamia* "To see herself escap'd from so sore ills" — it is idiomatic if not grammatical, and I am always on the side of idiom as against grammar.

I can't find "a doing" in my papers, but if it is there I can defend it as an archaism. Also Scott used the word in the singular.

But I by no means pretend to be an impeccable writer.

¹ The Society for Pure English was founded by Robert Bridges and a group of his friends in 1913 to protect the purity of the language and "in recognition of the need to arrive at some linguistic ideal, some standard of excellence by which the value of linguistic fashions can be judged and tested." Smith was a member and wrote some of its tracts.

* * *

TO EDWARD MARSH   December 2, 1935

I think we shall have some fun when we start our word-coining mint. Do make a note of any verbal needs as they occur to you, new names for things, or better ones for those for which the terms are awkward. I want names for *pensée* and *long short story,* also an English expression for *enfant terrible.* The world is full of such at present.

But my great ambition — the thing I am intriguing for — is to replace *anti-cyclone* by *halcyon.* I have consulted the Oxford Press about it, and they approve. Kenneth Sisam suggests *halcyon weather.* "A large halcyon is approaching our shores" — what a touch of poetry that would add to the weather broadcasts!

* * *

TO EDWARD MARSH   October 12, 1944

I am amusing my octogenarian ("don't need a geranium") leisure by indulging, more devotedly than ever in my old linguistic predilections and am even dreaming idly of setting up a private mint for coining words — a mint like the Baring-Ponsonby mint, in which I have reason to suspect you sometimes employed a counterfeiter's hand. I note what you say in your book about a *"Shelley-plain,"* and your wise shortening (an unpunishable crime) of that uncouth modern monstrosity the "inferiority complex" into an "inflex."

Last Saturday a few word-fanciers met here for a word-mongering confabulation — Desmond MacCarthy, Cyril Connolly and Rose Macaulay, and I wish you could have been with us. We all submitted words we had collected from old books or had ourselves invented. "Orchidaceous" for pansified young men was Desmond's contribution and "going-a-Pope-ing" (A-POPEING, my writing is so bad) was Rose Macaulay's descriptive name for the Rome-ward tendencies of so many of our friends.

I enclose a list of my suggestions and should be interested to know if any of them meet with your approval.

Old Coins from the Collection of L.P.S.

Crocodilean

Orageous

Chambering

Mayfair Jezebel (Thackeray)

Colossious — stronger than Colossal

Beaumond (Congreve)

Milver — name of someone who shares our admirations, ecstasies, and above all, our execrations. (Also a rhyme for the rhymeless word "silver.")

From the Mint of L.P.S. at Chelsea

Debretting — talking about the Lords one meets in the Beaumond.

Bougresses — the old Hostesses and great Ladies of the Beaumond.

An Abednego — one who has walked in that fiery furnace and has not been scorched.

Catjumping — discovering for one's secret delectation an old (or a new) writer or painter, and hearing next day the Bougresses and Social Climbers and Kensington Roarers, all shouting it on the stairs.

Sheepgoating — separating authors, painters, and all one's friends and acquaintances into right hand and (mostly) left hand pens.

From a Mint at Windsor

Cramthroating — one's friends with books.

Onways — the stories that in one's dotage one tells them much more than once.

Swimgloat — an eagle-hurried rapture into High Society after which it isn't easy to find one's feet.

A Cowper-Drink and an Antrim-Boat — describes interesting disillusions which are too esoteric to be easily explained.

Inflex — a most useful portmanteau-word for "Inferiority complex." (E. Marsh)

Shelley-Plain — a useful Baring expression for glimpse of a great man. (E. Marsh)

Gluebottom — a visitor who won't go away.

Coins Minted by Rose Macaulay

A-Popeing — to go a-popeing. To incline towards Rome.

Pence — for Pensées. Pansy has other floral uses.

Friends

Of all the means which wisdom uses to ensure happiness throughout life, by far the most important is the acquisition of friends.

— Epicurus, *Sovran Maxims*

The friends Smith enjoyed most were other writers. It was about them that he wrote with most feeling and to whom he sent his most spontaneous and stimulating letters, and these appear in various sections of this collection. Here are a few to show his feelings about some of these friends as persons and as writers. They cover a remarkable span: from Walt Whitman, who was born in 1819, to Hugh Trevor-Roper, who was born nearly a hundred years later.

Walt Whitman

Smith's sister Mary first heard of Walt Whitman in 1882, when she was a student at Smith College. Whitman's reputation was dubious after the publication of Leaves of Grass, *and he was then living in poverty in Camden, New Jersey, across the river from Philadelphia. Mary admired his poems, and during her Christmas holidays she determined to visit him, despite the disapproval of her family. The trip was a success. Whitman went home with her, met the family, and stayed a month. After that he was a regular visitor in the Smith house. Logan Smith's first mention of him is in an undated letter apparently written from Haverford College. There are three others about him written from New York in the fall and winter 1886–1887.*

TO HIS SISTER MARY   [Undated]

I am spending Sunday over here to study for examination, and this is the way I do it! I have indulged in a little W.W. today. I read his Memoranda[1] of the War . . . I cannot express to thee what I feel in words, but I know thee understands my enthusiasm for him. I have been reading and talking about nothing else, and have several converts already. I was very much interested in that book of John Burroughs[2] and so I tried to get a copy for myself. I could not find one but I ordered a man on Ninth Street to send to New York for one of the second edition. Yesterday I was in town and stopped in the store to see if they had got it and there was the old gentleman himself [Whitman] looking very natural, and wasn't it a coincidence? I told him about thee and myself, he seemed surprised that I liked his *Vistas*[3] and told me that thee and I and our friends were the only young people that understood him. He asked for thy address, which I gave him, and said he was going to send thee some things. He seemed as well as usual, and in parting said he would often like to have a chat with me. When I see him I never think of him as a grand poet, but simply as a dear old man. I first got interested in his poetry coming up in the train from Atlantic City, in about an hour my ideas on many subjects were entirely changed, especially the way I looked at vulgar and stupid people. Now they seem like beautiful souls temporarily uninviting in attire, of manners, habits, etc.

[1] *Memoranda During the War,* a prose work published in 1875.
[2] John Burroughs (1837–1921), writer of nature essays and friend of Whitman.
[3] *Democratic Vistas,* a prose pamphlet published in 1871 and containing earlier essays.

*   *   *

TO HIS SISTER MARY

I went to see Walt Whitman Sunday — he had been quite ill all the week before but was better Sunday and was sitting up and reading — but it made my heart weep to see him however, and somehow I got the impression that he was old, sick and alone. He insisted however that he was cheerful and said that he ought to be thankful that it was no worse. Do write to him as often as thee can and send him some books. He quite brightened up when I suggested sending him some. He only said they must be very trashy, as he did not feel much like reading anything else. When I told him that thee seemed very happy he said "That's good" over several times, more to himself than to me and in a tone that meant really *good* and gave the word the genuine old Saxon meaning which it doesn't generally have. He is the first person I have met so far since I have been here who really seemed interested in me and what I had been doing in Europe and didn't just ask a few polite questions and then regale me with a tale of their doings — as uninteresting to me of course as mine to them. I came away with the feeling that it wasn't so much ideas that he gave you, as a whole new point of view — *Weltan-schauung* — ideas in solution tho' not yet crystallized.

* * *

TO HIS SISTER MARY

I saw Mr. Whitman two weeks ago. He seemed much better and in good spirits and had just come in for a ride. I think his mind is as clear as ever though expression is a little difficult for him. It struck me that he was tired of being a poet and being literary and preferred new things and conversation that made no demands on his intellect.

* * *

I must tell thee about W.W.'s reception here. It was really a great success and he enjoyed it very much, I think. He sat in a big arm chair in the middle of a crowd of people and whoever came was taken up to be introduced by a man who has a jewelry shop in the Bowery. He generally got people straight, however, although he was heard to introduce an aristocratic young novelist of the Howells and James school named Bishop, with a pretty and bashful young wife, as Bishop the mind-reader.

It was a cosmos certainly, after a weird pair of spiritualists who came especially to present the poet with a copy of a religious *Philosophical Journal of Chicago* with an article marked in red on the religion of Lincoln and then came a fat *littérateur* from Boston who remarked in a loud voice "Mr. Whitman I have been waiting to meet you for years." Her voice sank into her boots on the "years" but W.W. rose to the occasion and asked her to sit down. However, all the literary swells were there and everyone was enthusiastic about him and his lecture. I am so glad he had this bit of hero worship at the end of his life. [Whitman was 68 at this time; he died in 1892 at 73.]

Henry James

Smith was one of a number of young men who admired Henry James and helped build the legend of The Master. He was a consistent reader of James's novels through the years, and valued his friendship. No one is quoted more often in Smith's letters. James wrote of him, in 1913, "Logan Pearsall Smith was just here with me for thirty-six hours and the tide of gossip between us rose high, he being a great master of that effect."

TO HIS SISTER ALYS

I met Henry James yesterday. Harold Russell invited me to meet his people, Lord and Lady Arthur Russell, at tea in his rooms and Henry James was there too. He is small and very French in his appearance and has a disagreeable, sneering way of talking. It is only his manner that makes people dislike him however, I think, for after I had talked to him for a while he seemed very much like Prof. [William] James. He said a number of clever things, most of which I have forgotten. In speaking of New York, however, he said that it was impossible to have a picturesque address there, and he told me that he had gone back to New York to live and be a good American citizen, but at the end of a year he had quietly packed up his few belongings and come away.

* * *

Lamb House, Rye, Sussex
TO HIS SISTER ALYS October 21, 1913

I got here safely yesterday about 6, leaving Ford at 2:30. Henry James met me very kindly, although it was wet and cold, and drove me up the hill to this charming old house — a panelled Georgian house, much the size of Ford, in a quiet corner of this little old red town. It is very neat and old-maidish and quiet and comfortable, and exactly the sort of place Henry James ought to live in. He seems old and delicate and rather melancholy and lonely, but he loves talking, and if you give him time for all his parentheses and qualifications and little touches, he gives you in return portraits of people and places and incidents that are quite like his writings. He sees everyone in a more or less tragic predicament — including himself — and it is all dramatic and lurid — though lurid isn't exactly the word. So far we have had the tragedies of Mrs. Humphrey Ward,[1] Mrs. Wharton,[2] and Sturges,[3] and I expect there is a rich feast to follow.

[1] Mary Augusta Ward (1851–1920), a prolific writer of popular English novels in the 1880s and 1890s.
[2] Edith Wharton was a friend of both Smith and Henry James.
[3] Jonathan Sturges (1864–1909), a Princeton graduate who spent much of his time in Europe and was in James's circle of friends. He once recalled to James a conversation with William Dean Howells in the Paris garden of James McNeill Whistler. Sturges had just arrived in Paris and asked Howells for advice and this, he told James, is what Howells said: "Oh, you are young, you are young — be glad of it: be glad of it and *live*. Live all you can; it's a mistake not to. It doesn't so much matter what you do — but live. This place makes it all come over me. I see it now. I haven't done so — and now I'm old. It's too late. It has gone past me — I've lost it. You have time. You are young. Live!" This gave Henry James the idea for *The Ambassadors*.

Ethel Sands (1873–1962), though American, was the daughter of an Edwardian London hostess, Mrs. Mahlon Sands. A remarkably versatile and accomplished woman, she was a talented painter and her interest in all the arts made her a pivotal figure in English cultural society in the first half of this century. Her friends were the most prominent artists and writers of the day, and she counted Henry James and Smith among them. Memoirists of her time describe her in superlatives; a fuller picture emerges in a letter Smith wrote to Hugh Trevor-Roper, page 117.

*　*　*

11 St. Leonard's Terrace

TO ETHEL SANDS　　　　　　　September 21, 1915

I see dear Henry now and then — he was ill for weeks and very miserable, but is in good form again. He lunched here last week to meet [George] Santayana, and gave us a display of his form that was simply magnificent. He was just a little naughty about the nation he has joined.

*　*　*

TO ETHEL SANDS

I have very sad news to tell you, which you have probably already heard. Poor Henry James is gravely ill — he had two strokes last Thursday and is partially paralyzed by them. He was struck down in the morning on getting out of bed, but fortunately could make his servants hear, and was put back to bed, and then the other stroke came that night. It was a question whether he would live . . . How wonderful he was at luncheon that day before you went! Mrs. Prothero[1] tells me that he hates death and would never allow it to be mentioned. It is very sad for him now. But he told me not long ago that he had no courage or desire to make an effort to live — age and isolation and the war had made him indifferent to everything.

[1] Fanny Prothero, the wife of George Prothero, editor of *The Quarterly Review,* was a Rye neighbor of James, a friend who helped him with household matters.

* * *

TO ETHEL SANDS

I haven't any good news to send you of poor Henry James — he has made a recovery from his pneumonia and pleurisy, and they are able to move him into his study where he can lie looking out of the window. But his mind gets no better — indeed seeems rather less clear than it was. It is very sad, and they haven't much hope for his recovery. But he has gleams now and then of his old wit, and is very amusing about his nurses, who worry him a good deal. He said the other day that they were all "claws and chirps." The other day in talking of some American cousins he said "what they really love is good dinners and bereavements."

I wonder if, like me, you sometimes get tired of being good? One isn't — at least I am not — made for keeping it up for long. I want to be lazy and spend money and travel and have good dinners, and I have had enough of margarine and porridge and philanthropy. But I suppose one would get still more tired of being bad — but I should like to try it for a bit. Miss Trevelyan and I are faithful to Elaine,[1] who has been going through the most awful troubles lately; as you perhaps know, she has quarrelled with Craig Kennedy, and although he rescues her time after time from rope and sewers and other dangers, she is still angry on account of the poisoned kiss, and treats him disgracefully. But fortunately the cinema world is one in which everything ends well and good-looking people are always good — so it is much to be preferred to the world in which we are living.

[1] The heroine of a celebrated serial film of the time.

* * *

11 St. Leonard's Terrace
TO ETHEL SANDS   February 29, 1916

You have no doubt seen that dear Henry died yesterday afternoon. He lost consciousness last Friday and never recovered it and died very peacefully. His case had been hopeless for a long time — apparently the clot of blood had destroyed part of his brain, and one can only be glad that his illness and discomfort are over. He is to be cremated on Friday. It's a great loss to feel that he is no longer in the world. I feel as if a great cathedral had disappeared from the skyline, a great country with all its civilization been wiped from the map, a planet lost to the solar system. Things will happen and he won't be there to tell them to, and the world will be a poorer and more meagre place. We shall all miss the charm and danger of our relation with the dear elusive man, the affectionate and wonderful talks, the charming letters, the icy and sad intervals, and the way he kept us all allured and aloof, and shone on us, and hid his light, like a great variable but constant moon.

Bertrand Russell

When Bertrand Russell proposed to Alys Smith in 1893 he was neither accepted nor rejected; it was not until the spring of 1894 that they became officially engaged. Meanwhile, Russell had written to Logan Smith to ask him his opinion of the marriage.

44 Grosvenor Road, London
TO BERTRAND RUSSELL   December 2, [1893]

Of course I know how matters stand, and naturally being as fond of my sister as I am, I do not regard your way of feeling as folly. And if you remain of the same mind after several years, I can assure you that I don't know of anyone who I should like better as a brother-in-law — nor indeed do I think there is anyone who would make a better husband for Alys. But sincerely I think you would make a mistake by engaging yourself too soon — but I dare say you don't intend to do that. One never knows what one will develop into, and anyhow the first few years after 21 should be given to self education, and the search for one's work, and marriage, or even a settled engagement, interferes sadly with all that.

Yes I *do* believe in you, Bertie, though the faculty for belief is not one of those most developed in me — only I shall believe more in your decision when I see that after a few years of good work and experience of the world you still remain the same. Win your spurs, *mon cher* — let us see that you are good and sensible — as indeed we believe you are — your friends all have the highest ideas of your ability and promise, only keep yourself free and interested in your work. Love should be the servant, not the master of life.

* * *

Fernhurst, Haslemere
TO HIS SISTER ALYS   July 15, 1902

Mariechen's[1] party on Sunday went off very well. Bertie was in great form and held the ears of the company. If one argues with him one begins to feel as one does in a dream, that one has gone out into public insufficiently clothed.

The summer congress for discussing the world in general seems to go on all day long now at Friday's Hill. Bertie's paradoxes sometimes seem to make the trees stand on their heads. B.B.[2] who roars like a lion among the mountains of Fiesole is as mild as a lamb on the hills of Fernhurst.

[1] This was the family nickname for Mary Berenson.
[2] Bernard Berenson was universally known as "B.B."

* * *

London
TO HIS SISTER MARY   January 17, 1903

I went to Bertie's lecture on Friday. It was very clear and intellectual and even witty, and was successful in every way. He is writing a good deal, and becoming quite a public man. It seems like using a razor to chop wood, but such people are necessary to the State, and a person like Bertie must be haunted by "ancestral voices prophesying war." He is not as yet a party politician, and I don't think he will stand for Parliament. But he is conscientious, public-spirited and likes excitement, so I suppose he will always be popping out of his cloister into the world.

* * *

2 Grove Street, Oxford
TO KARIN COSTELLOE   December 22, 1905

I follow the news of thy operation with great interest and sympathy — thee evidently will be famous for thy courage, and for the operation itself. Thee will be like Uncle Bertie, whose real renown is not due to his philosophy and his books, but to something that was once done to his teeth, which has made him so illustrious in the Dental World that he sometimes goes to exhibit his mouth to amazed and admiring dentists.

Helen Thomas Flexner

Mrs. Flexner (1872–1956) was Smith's first cousin and a daughter of Hannah Smith's sister Mary. Her relationship with Smith was a close one. She was interested in writing, and he wrote to her frequently about books. In 1940 she published A Quaker Childhood, the story of her family. Her husband was Simon Flexner (1863–1946), a noted physician, pathologist, and for many years director of the Rockefeller Institute for Medical Research.

I Tatti

TO HELEN THOMAS FLEXNER   February 12, 1902

I wish thee could have a picture in thy mind of this house, for it would be a charming picture — cypresses and statues, dark high forests and cactus behind, and in front the far blue mountains, and for music the church bells and mountain torrents. All the rooms look to the south, opening from long wide, white corridors; the light is softened by green shutters and there is everywhere quiet, order and priceless old furniture and pictures. So, life goes on, the work, joy, worry, grumble, gossip of the stream of life: floating on toward middle age together. Youth sometimes visits us, eager, generous, empty-headed youth — with what joy and even what envy alas we look at it, clutch at it. But for malicious middle age there is Horace Walpole's wicked comfort — wait a bit and the young of today will be on our side, pushed into middle age by a quicker-coming generation.

Berenson says that every period of life has its old age with its own sense of senile melancholy. The old age of boyhood was bad enough but the old age of the young man is the worst of all. So much goes, alas! the freshness of hope and sensation and that divine vague, romantic "perhaps" which shimmers in the background of every youthful prospect.

What remains? To take whatever the Muses or others give and, after all that is so much! The impersonal, contemplative pleasures, and then the peace of mind which youth has not — to enjoy whatever a kindly fortune may bestow.

[49]

Philip Morrell's[1] marriage — and I suppose it is this change — as change it must be — in an old and intimate friendship which has involved me in these sentiments . . . The marriage is certainly a romantic and interesting one. Lady Ottoline is a stately, beautiful, shy, lost Princess, seeking for goodness, happiness, salvation. Imagine taking into one's ordered, ironical life a noble, great-winged, grave-eyed bird like that! I grow giddy at the thought. As a rule I think of people who marry with detachment and a certain gratitude — it is they who provide us spectators with human drama — they play over for us the old familiar hackneyed interesting play. But when one's intimate friend marries it is different; one is dragged into the play one's self and given a part that is melancholy and ridiculous as well. When in *Trivia* I rashly asked of the fates what part I was to play on this old stage of the world, I did not, I admit, expect so prompt an answer. Ask no questions of the fates! 'tis a perilous adventure. However, I hope my part will be pleasanter than what one is tempted to fear at first. I find myself capable of believing in spite of the old experience of the world that a friend who marries is not lost.

[1] Philip Morrell (1871–1943), Smith's close friend from Oxford undergraduate days, was a lawyer and later a Liberal member of Parliament for South Oxfordshire. He was married in 1902 to Lady Ottoline Cavendish-Bentinck (1873–1938), whose salons in Bloomsbury and at her country house, Garsington, near Oxford, attracted the leaders of the intellectual *avant-garde* of England. She appeared in Smith's world when she married Morrell and later, in a bitter rift, when she had a celebrated affair with his brother-in-law, Bertrand Russell.

* * *

High Buildings, Haslemere
TO HELEN THOMAS FLEXNER   July 11, 1902

I am hoping that Philip Morrell and his wife will be living in this house for a few weeks this summer. They have already paid me a visit and she is as charming and friendly as anybody can be. When I see them, their youth, their good looks, their happiness in each other, it is like coming into a little of the sunshine of the bleak world; and I am stirred with thoughts of romance that would amuse thee. But when I am by myself my thoughts return to their old channels — I see either clouds blowing up to shut out the sunshine, or else the sunshine itself becomes to my mind a commonplace, foolish glare. This old utilitarian world has a trick of ensnaring people with romance into humdrum routines. But why should I croak? Certain things interest me, and others don't. I find a great deal to interest me in this world — the legal bliss of marriage is not one of them.

*　*　*

High Buildings, Haslemere

TO HELEN THOMAS FLEXNER April 15, 1903

Many thanks for thy charming letter, and the delightful news it contained [she had told him she was engaged to be married] — for it is delightful to have news of such a thing happening; and I am grateful to thee for believing that I would understand and not be too cynical to appreciate the wonder of it. Everything in our mortal condition can be made fun of, and life itself often looks ridiculous enough, but as one gets older one knows that it is not the satirists who have the best of it in the long run, but those who hear the great music, to whom the spring floods come, and who have the courage and richness of nature to accept the great gifts of life. I have my own little system of things, but it is only a personal one, suited to my own nature and I confess I look over my ledge on the stream of life with a certain envy on those in whose sails the great breeze is blowing, and who are sailing to new countries while I grow middle aged amid my pleasant but rather humdrum . . . [illegible] and what a difference at thy age (excuse the phrase) knowing life before and after, to wisely set out on this wise adventure with a wise and noble companion. Never class thyself with those foolish chance-arranged expeditions of boys and girls we laugh at, though from old custom the same music will be played and the same banners waved. I had already heard of the name of Dr. Flexner as a man of great distinction.

*　*　*

I must send greetings to the new arrival[1] in this remarkable world, and congratulations to thee. It must be a very strange and wonderful event — the strangest and most wonderful that can happen — and the news of it has given me curious and delightful and delicate thoughts. May the young imp be a nursling of the Muses, and a lover of immortal song, and may the stars shine kindly on him. Say what you will, it is a privilege to be born into this famous world, and he will, I am sure, be grateful. I should like to hear what he is like, and what plans thee has made for his future. Tell me how thee is settled, and what corner of quiet thee has found for thyself in uproarious New York.

I am settled happily in the solitude and autumnal sunshine of High Buildings, and am busy with my work and reading. I hope to get Wotton finished sometime soon, and when the old ghost is appeased, and the due funeral rites are performed, and the necessary dust is sprinkled, I can then wander through some of the delightful doors that seem to be standing open. Well, life is great fun, doesn't thee find it so? I like to think of the new human who is just starting out on that adventure.

[1] Mrs. Flexner's son, William Welch Flexner, was born on October 5, 1904. He became a distinguished mathematician and educator.

* * *

Thy charming letter (and no one's letters have a charm like thine) has been looking at me on my desk for some time, and I have been waiting for the moment, the mood, when I could dip in something out of the wells and springs of my life, to send thee in return for the cool and pleasant taste thee gives me of thy thoughts. Those wells and springs (small and shallow though they may be) have not yet dried up, and as long as I can sit by their banks in peace, and take my ease in my own oasis, I need not complain of the surrounding deserts, even if they seem, as one gets older, to stretch away to thirstier and more limitless horizons. I feel that my metaphor, once I had embarked on it, has led me further into pessimism than I meant to go, and I have done some injustice to the green surrounding hills, which indeed are most fresh and pleasant in this summer weather. However spiritual deserts (I can't escape the metaphor so it must have its way) I do discern; and sometimes return to my oasis thirsty and footsore and discouraged. But in the desert there are, after all, other oases not uninhabited by fellow creatures; one can find and visit them occasionally, or a messenger brings a cup of cold water from their springs. But the sandstorms that blow in on one now and then from the wastes of life, choking up the wells and spreading dust and desolation — we all, I suppose, are victims of these! and the ruin each time seems fatal and irremediable; yet the springs are cleansed and fill again, and the shimmer and joy of life comes back, and life is a great gift. I hold to that — a curious and marvelous experience; and though one pays for the privilege (and the finer one's taste, the more one pays) one must not repine. It's curious that though we desire happiness and success and contentment, we never envy happy or successful or contented people — we despise them rather; and I suppose the moral is that the great things of life are more truly with us in desire than in actual possession.

But I don't know why I am so didactic; I suppose it is thinking of life and the little human creature who is starting on this adventure under thy wondering care. If his eyes are already looking for things he cannot find, I hope they will never lose their expression; and I who have already gone a long way in the impossible search, can only send him a message to say that I do not yet wish to turn back, and have no envy of those who were contented with more comfortable ambitions.

I was much interested in all thee told me of thy life in New York, and I sincerely hope that better health will come to thee and that Simon will find a corner of peace and leisure in the midst of the whirlpools of New York. Busy and important as he is, he can't suffer from what not infrequently depressed the spirits of people like myself, who keep aloof from life —

the weighing of oneself in the balance and finding one is wanting. It is wonderful to live with the spirits of the great, but one must meet one's contemporaries to feel one's own value.

* * *

I have long been meaning to write to thee — my thoughts are often with thee and Simon. They rest there as in a haven after homeless flights across the American continent, and bring back olive branches in their beaks. And now I must send greetings to this young creature[1] of whom I have heard with so much interest. Tell him to love the best, and to hate the second-rate. I can't give him better advice.

Since my heavy book [the Wotton biography] was finished and out I have been rather pleasantly idle. I have however gone over some sonnets, and had them set up in type, and am sending thee a copy. I don't feel that they possess much real literary merit — the task is almost too impossible — but it has amused me very much writing them and I thought I would print though probably not publish them.

[1] James Thomas Flexner, who became a celebrated American historian, was born on January 13, 1908.

Gertrude Stein

In the summer of 1902 Gertrude Stein and her brother Leo were in England, where they met Mary and Bernard Berenson. They then went to Haslemere for a visit with the Smith family. By 1913 Gertrude Stein was living in Paris and had published the first of her books. She was also in that year trying to get some of her writings published in England, and with that in mind she paid another visit to London. She had already written two of her portraits in prose, one of the American novelist and dramatist Constance Fletcher (1853–1938), and the other of Mabel Dodge Luhan (1879–1962), patron of many writers and artists. Miss Stein found to her surprise that one person in England who admired her work was Logan Pearsall Smith. "He went quite off his head about your Portrait," she wrote Mabel Dodge, "and never goes anywhere without it and wants to do an article for the English Review." *Another admirer of Miss Stein in England was Smith's cousin Emily Dawson, who was trying to get the Dodge portrait published.*

TO EMILY DAWSON

14 Merton Street, Oxford
January 22, 1913

Thank you for your card. I should like to see the portrait of Constance Fletcher and will return it carefully.

I have heard from the editor of the *English Review* that he would like to see some of this prose, so perhaps you will ask Miss Stein to send him a specimen — the Mabel Dodge or anything else and he may like to publish it or an article about it. His address is 17-21 Tavistock Street, Covent Garden, W.C. In writing she had better mention my name.

I should like to meet Miss Stein, if she will be in London next Wednesday or Thursday.

*　*　*

TO HIS SISTER MARY

Ford Place, Arundel
February 19, 1913

Thee asks about my impression of Gertrude Stein. I only saw her once at tea at Emily's. She seemed to me as fat as ever, but better dressed and generally improved in appearance. She is amusing and jolly and tells good stories about people. Her post-Impressionistic prose is fantastically absurd, of course, but to invent anything so crazy shows a kind of originality — There has certainly never been anything else like it.

*　*　*

TO GERTRUDE STEIN

I sent on your manuscript to the Oxford paper, but the editor writes that he is afraid it is rather too long for them, as their paper is not a very large one. They would very much like however, to have something shorter, and have asked me to ask you whether this is possible. They suggest printing the portrait of Miss Fletcher. Shall I send this on to them, or will you let them have something else? I don't suppose it would do to print Miss Fletcher's name, but they might print the initials C. F.

I am going abroad next week for a month or two, but if they may have the Miss Fletcher, and you will let me know at once, I can forward it to them before I start. I have the manuscript here. If however you wish them to have anything else, it would be better to send it direct to the Editor, *Oxford Fortnightly,* Holywell Press, Oxford.[1]

[1] *The Portrait of Constance Fletcher* appeared in Gertrude Stein's book *Geography and Days* in 1922 and *The Portrait of Mabel Dodge at the Villa Curonia* was first published by Miss Dodge herself in an edition of 300 copies in 1912. In 1934 it appeared in Miss Stein's *Portraits and Prayers,* and it was also included in her *Selected Writings* in 1946.

Virginia Woolf

Smith himself described this friendship in an article he wrote for the Orion *magazine in 1945:*

> *Founded years ago on a family alliance, and nourished by a certain liking for each other's way of writing, a curious kind of relationship had blossomed cactus-like, between Virginia Woolf and myself; one of those minglings of friendship and malice which add to the exasperation of life, but still more to its interest. Now and then we wrote to each other, and now and then I would go to see her. She would seem embarrassed, shy, almost hostile, but always polite in her stately way. . . .*
>
> *Still Mrs. Woolf and I were friends, or at least enemy-friends, a good many years, and such friendships I enjoy*

almost as much as warmer attachments; and even after I had
become conscious of a deepening chill in the air when we
met, we wrote to one another now and then.

A specific cause for at least one of the chills is found in
letters they exchanged. In January 1924 Mrs. Woolf wrote to
Jacques Raverat, the French painter, that she had been "engaged in a great wrangle with an old American called Pearsall
Smith on the ethics of writing articles for high rates for fashion
papers like Vogue." She said Smith felt it was demeaning, that
she should write for prestige and for posterity but what she
wanted was money.

Smith's side of the controversy is found in a short explanation he attached to their exchange of letters on the subject
when he sent them to the Library of Congress. "If authors of
promise," he said, "habitually wrote for trashy people, they
would very likely end by writing trash themselves."

Several of the following letters refer to this disagreement.

11 St. Leonard's Terrace

TO VIRGINIA WOOLF   January 26, 1925

No, I had seen nothing of yours in *Vogue,* and didn't know
you had written for it when I mentioned the subject. But I
feel sure that your spoon is long enough and made [of] such
finely tempered metal that you can sup with Miss Todd[1] without damage. It was the younger writers I was thinking of who
perhaps are less efficiently equipped. I went away on Saturday
feeling myself terribly respectable and *bien-pensant.* I think
I must get myself a frock coat and try to get into the
Athenaeum. However, if one is a prig, I suppose one can't
help it; it is best to abound in one's own sense, and I cannot
help grieving, instead of being amused, to see Bloomsbury
descend from the heights and scatter its pearls in Mayfair. If
the banner of fastidious discriminations doesn't hang out on
those heights, where is one to look for it these days?

I am making enquiries about American fiction and will let
you know the results. In the meantime I am sending you two
books of Sherwood Anderson, who is regarded, and rightly, I

think, as the best of the new school. I should look at the autobiography first, especially the Epilogue, and then at the volume of stories.[2] He impresses me as having a real talent, and a real desire to get closer to the texture of life, though style and charm are wanting, and I find the uneasy national consciousness and inferiority complex a bore. I have read a book by Willa Cather which I liked . . . Henry James used to say that the best story writer in America was a Negro, William Du Bois,[3] but the fact was hushed up on account of color prejudice. I see that his *The Souls of Black Folk* is in the London Library. I don't think however that Harper would welcome his praise. I am told that one oughtn't to touch Hearst's magazines with a pair of tongs. Harper's is of course perfectly all right.

[1] Dorothy Todd, editor of British *Vogue* from 1922 to 1926.
[2] *A Story-Teller's Story,* Anderson's autobiography, was published in 1924. Smith had already mentioned that he was sending Mrs. Woolf a book of Anderson short stories, *The Triumph of the Egg.*
[3] William Edward Burghardt (W.E.B.) Du Bois (1868–1963), writer, editor, and teacher, was trained as a sociologist and wrote many books to promote understanding of the Negro in America. *The Souls of Black Folk* (1903) was one of his best known.

* * *

11 St. Leonard's Terrace

TO VIRGINIA WOOLF   1925

I don't think I at all deserve the luck to have escaped your clever and most justifiable trap[1] —, indeed the fine sentiment of your letter makes me feel that I owe you and Bloomsbury an apology. I did not realize the noble and unmercenary motives for writing in the fashion papers which you allege. In common with the base-minded world, I had guessed at quite other incentives. But now I withdraw, I apologize. If you believe that it is one's duty to culture to corroborate the activities of Todd, though in my stuffy way I may question the validity of your principles, I cannot but applaud your adherence to them and admire Bloomsbury more than ever for its willingness to suffer this painful misunderstanding I have hinted at in the performance of its noble, if lucrative duty to culture.

If, as you say, *Vogue* doesn't as a rule pay more than the high-brow weeklies and if, as you also very rightly suggest, it is better for young writers to be highly paid in order to reduce their needed journalistic efforts to a minimum, I cannot but feel that their arguments have what I may call a cumulative effect which is overwhelming.

[1] Mrs. Woolf related in a letter to Smith (January 25, 1925) that she had inadvertently set a trap for him by sending to *Vogue* an article she had intended for the highbrow *Nation*.

* * *

St. Leonard's Terrace
TO VIRGINIA WOOLF   November 2, [1932]

Thanks for your letter. Do not be alarmed by the thought that I am proffering an olive branch. I only want to say that I don't think I have ever been really hostile to Bloomsbury. I have always thought, and sometimes said (to the intense annoyance of my hearers) that I regarded Bloomsbury as the only group of free spirits in the English-speaking race. I may have mocked at Bloomsbury, because mockery is my favorite pastime, and also perhaps (to take a darker peep into that dark cabinet, the human heart) because I was not admitted to its conclaves. That I have told funny stories about it is possible, nor is it utterly inconceivable that I may have invented one or two. I see in the tract of my conversion (I have found a copy)[1] that my little sister's first prayer, when we kneeled together, was as follows: "O Lord, please make little Logan a good boy and don't let him tell any more lies."

Her little friend then prayed, "Lord please give Logan a new heart," and Logan earnestly echoed her prayer in these words, "Lord Jesus, please give me a new heart."

It would appear, however, that the prayers of these little girls, and of my little (and better) self have not been really answered, so I must get on as best I can with only my old heart.

So there it is, and there it must remain. I know from my own feelings how justly critics resent criticism, and mockers being mocked.

[59]

I have been reading with great interest what you say about Fulke Greville[2] in your book [*The Common Reader, Second Series, 1932*]. I read his aphorisms some years ago; they are (like all collections of this kind, except those of Rochefoucauld) of a devastating dullness, but having a perverted taste for this kind of literature, I copied out a few which I thought might interest you:

> Those who listen to themselves are not listened to by others.
> A proud man never shows his pride so much as when he is civil.
> To divest one's self of some prejudices, would be like taking off one's skin to feel better.

It was supposed at the time, I believe, that Mrs. Greville wrote these aphorisms; but this I can hardly believe, since no woman except George Eliot has been mistress of the delicate art.

[1] This is described in the next two letters.
[2] Richard Fulke Greville, an eighteenth-century aristocrat, published *Maxims, Characters, and Reflections Critical, Satirical and Moral* in 1756. Virginia Woolf referred to its author as a man who "lived dashingly, daringly, with perpetual display."

* * *

St. Leonard's Terrace

TO VIRGINIA WOOLF   1932

I am thinking of following your example (I am reading your essays with the enchantment with which I read all your writings) in collecting together my various essays in a volume which Constable have agreed to publish. As one of these, "The Prospects of Literature," was printed by you, I wonder if I could come to some arrangement with the Hogarth Press about it? I would gladly purchase the unsold copies if I might recover the copyright in this manner, and thus your books would be relieved of a bothersome little account.

My *Stories from the Old Testament*[1] which you also published is now, I believe, out of print. Does this give me the right to print them again? I should like to do so, as I find they have helped many to find salvation, and I have thus been carrying on my family trade of saving souls, and hope to wear these diamonds in my heavenly crown. Of rubies I shall have an abundance, since a tract published by my father long ago, called *How Little Logan Was Brought to Jesus*, recounts how my sister Mary and a little friend of hers took me at the age of four into my father's study and accomplished, by means of earnest prayer, my conversion. This tract had an enormous circulation at the time, and produced an especially powerful effect on the Red Indians of the West, who were quite unable to withstand it.

[1] This fifty-three-page pamphlet published by the Hogarth Press consisted of eleven Bible stories retold with a contemporary ring. They were about Moses, David and Goliath, Jezebel, Jonah, and other characters who lent themselves to these somewhat wry reinterpretations.

* * *

TO VIRGINIA WOOLF
11 St. Leonard's Terrace
November 12, 1932

Your letter gave me great pleasure, and I like to cling to the belief that it was an olive branch, as indeed my own letters were, though I mingled a little bitter myrrh with them, so that you could take them in another sense, if you preferred. But the things I said about Bloomsbury and my regret at never seeing you were not in the least ironical, and came from the truest corner of that unsanctified heart, which, in spite of all the praying, I have never been able somehow to change for a better one. So some day I do hope you will let me come and see you. Why, as you say, shouldn't we mock each other before each other's faces? I love mockery so much that I am delighted when I am myself its subject; one's own vanities, humiliations I find a delicious subject for conversation. Things said of me behind my back I don't enjoy, and don't listen to them.

I am sorry that you aren't well; I spend a good deal of my time in a dull kind of invalidism, so that I can feel sympathy with you. But these spells end; one does emerge sooner or later from the dark tunnel, and I hope that this will soon happen to you. In the meantime, I have been copying out for you the tract of my conversion, or I should have written sooner. But just when I had finished making my copy, the Poltergeist or little devil which hides my pens, pencils, scissors, and spectacles every day, stole the neat little booklet, hid it in the chaos of non-existence which lies so close around each of us, and I can't find it anywhere, though I have searched every conceivable place a hundred times. I thought it might be a comfort and means of help to you in your illness, and shall now have it type-written at once, and send you a copy. I think it must be reprinted though I can hardly flatter myself that you will undertake the task.[1] But since it saved so many Red Indians in its time, might it not possibly help to salvation some of the Apaches and *jeunes féroces* of a region of London which I shall not name. I have a charming photograph of the holy little Logan which would make a delightful illustration for it.

Speaking of Bloomsbury (but have I been speaking of it?) I think the Irish saying might be quoted, "Distant cows have long horns," for I have never seen the long horns which you appear to have discerned across the intervening regions of Mayfair, while you say that the horns which we see so formidably looming in Bloomsbury are equally non-existent. Perhaps when we meet we shall turn out to be the harmless, hornless creatures, with nothing but the most friendly feelings for each other. But one admission I will make; Chelsea is a little infected by its proximity to Mayfair; over it hangs the stern verdict which I expressed in my little book of aphorisms as follows:

You cannot be both fashionable and first rate.

Not that we are really fashionable in Chelsea, but we want to be, and you don't.

I met the other day a beautiful and fashionable young queen of Mayfair who was, she told me, passionately devoted to books, and who said that she always heard and believed that Chelsea and Bloomsbury were one and the same kingdom, with Rebecca West as its queen. Perhaps this is the ultimate truth; it will at any rate serve as a pin-prick with which to end this letter.

¹ It was not reprinted by the Hogarth Press but was reissued in 1934 in a limited edition by Robert Gathorne-Hardy and Kyrle Leng at the Mill House Press.

*   *   *

TO VIRGINIA WOOLF   December 1, 1932

I should love to come and see you. I will bring some polished shafts from Chelsea, and hope you will have some ready from the armory of Gordon (or Gorgon) Square. But I shall be much too timid to start the conflict, so you must strike first, if you want a fight. But why should we fight after all? Why shouldn't we all love each other?

600 mss. to read a year! The thought staggers me out of my Christian waking. But I think I have an explanation. I met the other day a female wielder of the pen, called Helen Simpson, who told me that she had contracts to write in the next year:

1. An enormous novel, dealing with religion *au fond*.
2. Series of broadcast talks on food, with pamphlet.
3. A life of Lady Jane Grey (200 Pounds paid in advance).
4. A translation of several volumes of *Le Tableau de Paris*.
5. A large compendium for housewives on food, clothing, dress-making, upholstering, the care of drains, with hints on children, and how to keep husbands at home.
6. A life of Captain Cook.
7. A detective story in collaboration with Clemence Dane, the intervals to be filled with lectures and articles for the *Spectator*.

Now my theory is (I may be wrong) that the books you read are all written by this Helen Simpson, who out-writes you and out-runs you in the glorious race of glory — that she writes on faster than you can read. Am I right?

I will not end this letter with a pin-prick, which is after all a horrid way of writing, but with a perfectly irrevelant thought

[63]

which occurred to me this morning. Here it is: one of the sayings of Little Logan, "If you are losing your leisure, look out, you may be losing your soul."

* * *

TO VIRGINIA WOOLF   December 1, 1933

The Pronouncing Committee of the BBC (of which I am a member) decided yesterday to enlarge its numbers, and would I think feel highly honored if you would consent to join it. We want a woman on the committee and ought of course to have one (or more); and who could "voice" her sex better than you?

As you may perhaps hesitate about taking on this task, I thought I would write to tell you that the task is really a light one — the committee only meets for a couple of hours about twice a year. Bernard Shaw is the chairman, there are a few professors and lexicographers, Lascelles Abercrombie and myself. The committee was started by Robert Bridges. The meetings are good fun and no one need attend if they don't feel like it. Deciding on the pronunciation of special words isn't perhaps a matter of immense importance, but I hope — and believe — that the committee will come before long to undertake the more interesting task of providing — or at least suggesting — names for the new inventions, new ways of thought and feeling which come to birth continually and have to have baptismal names. Writers with some sense of language would often stand as godfathers in the past but now the naming of these brats is left to the newspapers, or what is worse, the men of science. Hence the horrors and cacophonies of our modern vocabulary. It may be possible to remedy — or at least to mitigate — this calamity and I hope you feel like lending a hand in this pious work.[1]

[1] Mrs. Woolf at first agreed to serve but withdrew a few months later, writing to Smith that she had never been on a committee in her life and felt it was too late to begin.

Robert Bridges

*Bridges (1844–1930) was one of the leading poets of his time,
author of twenty volumes of verse, and poet laureate from 1913
until his death. He was one of the writers Smith admired most,
and they worked together on tracts for the Society for Pure
English, of which Bridges was a founder. The two men had
met when Bridges sent Smith a letter of congratulations when
Trivia was first published.*

Oxford

TO HIS SISTER ALYS   May 12, 1913

I had a very pleasant visit to the Bridges, and have just descended in a pouring rain to Oxford. The Bridges were very
nice, full of leisure and talk about books, and the leisurely
atmosphere of the house is charming — there is only a serious
lack of bedroom curtains, and breakfast is at 8.

Bridges is full of his fads — classical metres, and the way
the Psalms are sung in churches — he sat a long time this
morning with his feet way up over his head, singing me the
Psalms of David, while I tried to do a little work.

*When Bridges was at Eton he was a friend of a remarkable
young man named Digby Mackworth Dolben, who wrote a
few fine lyric poems and died in 1867 at the age of nineteen.
In 1911 Bridges collected the poems and published them,
along with a Memoir of the young poet. "When his early
death endeared and sanctified his memory," Bridges wrote,
"loving grief would generously grant him the laurels he had
never won."*

Ford Place, Arundel

TO ROBERT BRIDGES   November 6, 1911

As one of the readers (I hope there will be many) of your
book about Dolben, I feel that I must thank you most gen-
uinely for the privilege and pleasure of making the acquaintance of so charming a person, and so remarkable a poet.
Your memoir makes him very real and living and lovable —
I feel exactly as if I had met him and had enjoyed his charm-

[65]

ing and fantastic companionship. I think you have given the portrait, and the picture of Eton life, probably better than you imagine, from some of the things you say — I cannot tell you how much the book has been in my mind, ever since I read it, and I shall hope eagerly for some more specimens of your biographic art. The poems too are a great acquisition — I knew nothing of them before, and some of them are very beautiful and haunting — it seems quite incredible that a boy of eighteen could have written them. No. 49 I have read a great many times — it is amazing. The book is a great treasure and lovers of these things will be very grateful to you for your pious act of friendship.

We are settled now in this beautiful old house (red brick, walled-in and panelled) in an open, lonely country between the downs and the sea. There is a great deal of wind and sky and the seashore is not far off.

* * *

TO ROBERT BRIDGES   October 31, 1913

I sent Henry James your book on Dolben and have had a long letter in return about it, which I amuse myself in copying out in the hope that it will interest you also:

"The disclosure and picture of the wondrous young Dolben have made the liveliest impression on me, and I find the personal report of him very beautifully and tenderly, in fact just perfectly done. Immensely must one envy him the possession of such a memory — recovered and restated, sharply rescued from the tooth of time, after so many piled-up years. Extraordinarily interesting I think the young genius himself, by virtue of his rare special gift, and even though the particular preoccupations out of which it flowered, their whole note and aspect, have in them for me something almost positively antipathetic. Uncannily, I mean, does the so precocious and direct avidity for all the paraphernalia of a complicated ecclesiasticism [Dolben's poems reflected his intensely religious feelings] affect me — as if he couldn't possibly have come to it, or as we say, 'gone in for it' by experience, at that age — so that there is in it a kind of implication of the in-

[66]

sincere, the merely imitational, the cheaply 'romantic.' However, he was clearly born with that spoon in his mouth, even if he might have spewed it out afterwards — as one wonders immensely whether he wouldn't. In fact, that's the interest of him — that it's the privilege of such a rare young case to make one infinitely wonder how it might or mightn't have been for him — and Bridges seems to me right that no equally young case has ever given us ground for so much wonder (in the personal and aesthetic connection). Would his 'ritualism' have yielded to more life and longer days, and his quite prodigious, but so closely associated gift have yielded *both* that (as though indissolubly mixed with it)? Or would a big development of inspiration and form have come? Impossible to say of course — and evidently he could have been but most fine and distinguished, whatever should have happened. Moreover it is just as we have him, and as Bridges has so scrupulously given him that he so touches and charms the imagination — and how instinctive poetic mastery was of the essence, was the most rooted of all things in him, a faculty or mechanism almost abnormal, seems to me shown by the thinness of his letters compared with the thickness of his verse.

"But how can one talk, and how can one be anything but wrapped for our delightful uncertainty, in the silver mists of morning, which one mustn't do so much as want to breathe upon too hard, much less clear away? They are an immense felicity to him, and leave him a most particular little figure in the great English roll. I go sometimes to Windsor and the very next one I shall peregrinate over to Eton on the chance of the sight of his portrait."

*   *   *

11 St. Leonard's Terrace
TO ROBERT BRIDGES   December 14, 1925

I am absorbed in my study of Italian words — practically our whole vocabulary of painting, sculpture, music comes from Italy, and architecture as well, also a large element of our terms on banking, war, horsemanship and the theatre. I hope to write an essay on the subject, which I will send you on the chance that it may do for a tract.

Your book of *New Poems* has been a great regale to me (to use a charming word that is dying out). Some of them I already know — others are a fresh delight, especially "Cheddar Pinks" and "The Tramps": this latter has an exquisite, subtle, haunting beauty and surprise that fills my thoughts. You have added those footsteps and voices to the consciousness of the world — the echo of them will never die. 1921 was certainly an *annus mirabilis* for your readers.

* * *

TO KENNETH CLARK
I Tatti
February 13, 1926

I am very glad you liked Robert Bridges and your mention of his gate reminds me to give you a warning of the utmost importance. *That gate must be carefully shut* on entrance and departure — the consequences otherwise may be of the gravest nature. Bridges, like another friend of ours, is fond of giving free exercise to the more superficial layers of his cerebrum, and talks a good deal of intolerant nonsense through his old and shabby hat; but his mind is really of an exquisite quality and when he seriously applies it to any subject the results are of the utmost value. Its purity, and his intolerance of moral failings, should be less of a drawback to virtuous youth, than it is to the older laxity of people like Roger Fry and myself. There is however only one serious quarrel between Bridges and myself — a latent quarrel since we have never really had it out — he is not a man with whom one can argue with impunity. He is against the kind of prose you and I like so much, he disapproved of my *Treasury* (though my own writing I think he has always liked) and he despises and execrates (or, used to) Sir Thomas Browne. Is not this curious? I wish I understood it. It isn't possible, no, it can't be possible that he is right.

Speaking of my *Treasury* (save for its misprints, how good it really is!) I have been looking at the passage you suggest. I agree with you about Johnson's letter and the passage from Pater is exquisite. I feel bitterly ashamed that I missed it.

Lytton Strachey's *Queen Victoria* should also, I suppose, be added though it is a stunt piece and suffers from Lytton's great defect, a poverty and slight commonness of diction.

* * *

11 St. Leonard's Terrace

TO ROBERT BRIDGES   November 2, 1929

I hope you are pleased with the great success of your poem[1]; everyone seems most enthusiastic about it, and I think it greatly to the credit of the reading public that they should appreciate its value and importance. For my part I read and re-read it with great interest and pleasure and, I hope, profit. In the chaos of modern thought and our general bewilderment, I could hardly have believed so broad a survey of life — seen from so serene an outlook — was possible for a modern writer, and I am — as many thousands must be — very grateful to you for it.

I know, of course, very little about metre, but your verse seems to me to justify itself in the reading, and be just the right medium for what you have to say — it serves admirably for the exposition of your thoughts and soars on ample wing to great heights of poetry, and adds a new lustre and a new music to English verse.

A critical estimate however in these matters is beyond my capacity. I can only try to express to you my admiration of the poem and my pleasure in reading it, and my delight that the great undertaking has reached so triumphant a conclusion.

[1] *The Testament of Beauty,* a long poem in which Bridges described his Platonic philosophy of life.

* * *

Big Chilling, Warsash

TO MRS. ROBERT BRIDGES   April 23, 1930

Your sad note prepared me for the news in yesterday's paper [of Bridges' death]. I am sure you know how constantly my thoughts have been with you and with how deep a sympathy.

The loss to the rest of us and to the world is irreparable — so splendid a figure, and so noble a life, we shall never know again, and the world will seem a poorer place for all who knew him. His long and kind friendship for me will always be one of the proudest of my memories, and the pride and pleasure I took in cooperating with him, up to my small ability, in his schemes is something I can never forget.

Since the end was bound to come, there is something splendid in its coming as it did, just when his great work was finished and he had crowned his career with this glorious last achievement. Life sometimes seems mean and poor, but his name will live to remind us that it need not be so — that it can be fine and disinterested and wholly devoted to noble aims.

I do hope it is some comfort to you to know how immensely you assisted and encouraged him in every way, and how completely he depended upon your help and fine judgment. If the world's debt to him is great, its debt to you is a great one also, for he would not have accomplished half he did, if you had not been, not only ready, but also able to assist him.

George Santayana

Smith was at Harvard with Santayana but did not know him until years later. Santayana started publishing the books of philosophy for which he is best known in the late 1890s and the early 1900s. By 1912 he had left America and was living in Europe, mainly in Italy, and it was then that he met Smith, who became one of his most ardent admirers.

TO ETHEL SANDS   February 27, 1916

I have been in Oxford for a few days for a change, staying with the Bridges and the Raleighs. I saw something of Santayana, who is now settled there, and means to make Oxford his home, as far as he has a home anywhere. He leads his delightfully detached life exactly in the fashion he likes, and says that if it wasn't for the war he would never have been so happy. He sees almost no one and, like a beautiful and subtle fish, successfully eludes all the nets spread to capture him.

* * *

Palazzo Borghese, Rome
TO HIS SISTER MARY   March 22, 1926

I went to see Santayana yesterday — he seems fat and cheerful, though he says he is growing deaf and old, and finds it difficult to write. But he doesn't seem to mind. He has two nice rooms at the Hotel Bristol, lunches at a restaurant, goes to sit in the Pincio, then comes home and puts on his dressing gown and dines in his own rooms. He thinks he may go eventually to live with his sisters in Avila — England, he says, has become too Americanized for him.

* * *

11 St. Leonard's Terrace
TO HIS SISTER MARY   March 17, 1930

I am returning the letters thee sent me. Santayana's letter would be a sad one, if I didn't think his pretense of decrepitude is only his fun — people who have seen him in Rome say that his mind is as clear and delightful as ever. But he certainly has become very reluctant to form or renew any human relationship. He has found his own kind of happiness, and that is after all no inconsiderable achievement.

* * *

11 St. Leonard's Terrace
TO GEORGE SANTAYANA   January 16, 1938

I hope the years have treated you as kindly as they have me; I was indeed pretty ill and in bed all last winter and came near to ending my unimportant fate; but the illness was not unpleasant and though it has left me in a somewhat damaged condition, I can still crawl out when the sun shines and when it doesn't, I can read all day long. I suffer indeed from periods of depression (being of the depressive manic type) but these

are followed by glorious outbursts of euphoria, in which everything seems delightful, and above all I feel, like the aged
archbishop of Granada that I can write, and have no Gil Blas[1]
at hand to tell me what I am writing is drivel.

One curious consequence of this has been that I have been
given a sip of that poisoned cup (but what is poison at our
age?) of American success at which you quaffed so deeply a
year or two ago. [Santayana's novel, *The Last Puritan*, was a
best-seller in America in 1936.] *The Atlantic Monthly* has
been printing some reminiscences of my boyhood and youth,
which seem to have roused such interest that their readers are
now clamoring for more. With my inspired archepiscopal pen
I am pleased to continue the record of my happy youth in the
golden age before the war and naturally the question of ex-
patriates has to be discussed. And this brings me to the occasion
of my writing to you now. You may remember that sixteen
years ago I went to the Johns Hopkins hospital at Baltimore
for an operation on that humble organ, the human bladder,
and wrote you the moan from that hospital of a returned expatriate who finds little comfort in returning to the land of his
birth. To that no doubt foolish moan you kindly returned me
a wise and consoling answer, which I have always preserved
and which, if you would allow me to incorporate in my reminiscences would give them great lustre and distinction. I
should not mention your name, if you prefer not to have it
mentioned. [The letter did appear anonymously in *Unforgotten Years*.]

[1] Hero of Alain-René Lesage's eighteenth-century picaresque novel,
L'Histoire de Gil Blas de Santillane.

Shaw and the Webbs

*George Bernard Shaw and Beatrice and Sidney Webb, co-
founders of the socialist Fabian Society, were frequent guests
in the circles in which Smith and his family moved.*

Big Chilling, Warsash, Hampshire

May 25, 1917

I am down here for Whitsuntide with the Webbs and Bernard
Shaw. It's the most ideal weather, and the place is delicious,
with the blue sea beyond the apple blossoms and the exquisite
air and sun. I wish thee knew what Chilling is like now, and
had a picture of it to hang in thy imagination. The Webbs are
always interesting and easy to get on with, and Shaw is a
gentle, egotistical talkative old creature — completely non-
aesthetic, who doesn't belong to our world at all, and just a
little of a bore. Still he is nice and human and friendly.

*   *   *

Big Chilling

TO HIS SISTER MARY   April 25, 1919

It is adorable down here, and the Spring more impossibly
beautiful than ever. The Webbs work away like beavers, but
are pleasant company when we see them. If the social revolution comes in a peaceable and rational way here, it will be
thanks to them more than to anybody. It was Sidney Webb
who averted a coal and railway strike that might have brought
on civil war, and devised this means of open exposure of
conditions and profits which has had such a profound effect
here. The defenders of private property and the present in-
dustrial system are singing in a very different key since the
revelations of the Coal Commission.

Cyril Connolly

*An early Smith protégé, Connolly (1903–1974) was a grad-
uate of Eton and Oxford and became a distinguished editor
and critic. He wrote for the* New Statesman *and* Nation, *was
a co-founder and editor of the English literary review* Horizon,
and chief book reviewer for the London Sunday Times. *His
best-known books were* Enemies of Promise *and* The Unquiet
Grave.

[73]

TO HIS SISTER MARY   June 30, 1926

I think I will spend my Lloyd George bet in helping, or trying to help, a young Oxford man about whom one of the
Balliol dons has written to me. They considered him at Balliol
one of their most brilliant scholars, but having a passion for
literature and Mediterranean travel, he did badly in the
schools, and is now thrown upon the world with great literary
ambitions, but not a penny. As I want someone to act as an
occasional secretary in finishing some jobs I have on hand —
among others a volume of Little Essays from Hazlitt, I thought
I would try him, especially as Kenneth Clark, who knows him
well, recommended him to me most highly as almost the most
brilliant and promising of his friends. He came to see me
yesterday — a little creature and as ugly as an ape, but full
of the things he wants to write. I have given him a job to see
how he will do it — without however great expectations, as
I don't believe in the younger generation. However, it is nice
to be able to give someone a chance.

* * *

11 St. Leonard's Terrace

TO HIS SISTER MARY   November 14, 1926

Connolly has made great friends with Desmond MacCarthy
who lectures him on his idleness — rather like Satan re-
proving sin! Desmond has now made Connolly go down to
Chilling to do some work. He wants to get a book out of him.
Connolly certainly is very original and clever, but he isn't one
of the world's workers.

Edith Wharton

*Smith met Edith Wharton in 1903, when she was visiting at
a villa in Italy near the Berensons. Theirs was a steady and
enduring friendship. Mrs. Wharton (1862–1937) published
many successful novels, notably* The House of Mirth *(1905),*
Ethan Frome *(1911), and* The Age of Innocence *(1920).*

TO EDITH WHARTON

I have enjoyed reading *The Gods Arrive* immensely, and must thank you very sincerely for giving me that pleasure. I'm not sure that it isn't your finest and most powerful work — the tragic tension produced by Vance's infatuation is presented in a masterly fashion, and you do make me feel his genius, which nobody else who has written about a genius has ever done before.

Here is a little linguistic problem on which you, or some one of your French literary friends may be able to throw a light. De Quincey, in his essay on Shakespeare, says "Few French authors, if any, have imparted one phrase to the colloquial idiom," and he mentions in contrast the enormous number of familiar phrases, images and turns of speech of Shakespeare's mintage with which the English language, written and colloquial, is enriched. Surely Molière added idioms to the French language. Have any other writers done so?

Jane Clark is still awaiting her double event.[1] I think her offspring are perhaps reluctant to emerge into the world in its present condition. They are waiting until the world crisis is over. Do you remember the story (I think Plutarch tells it) of the famous infant of Saguntum,[2] who was being born when the Carthaginians were sacking that city, and after a cursory glance, exclaimed, "Good heavens! this isn't at all the sort of world I want to be born into," and immediately drew back and died? I think modern infants must feel like that, especially when they hear of D. H. Lawrence, and the rage for Katherine Mansfield, which however, as I wrote you, I am hoping you will stop.

[1] Jane and Kenneth Clark's twins, Colin and Colette, were born in 1932.
[2] Saguntum was a city in Spain destroyed by Hannibal in the second Punic war, 219 A.D.

* * *

TO ROBERT GATHORNE-HARDY

I am trying to work myself up to an heroic deed — nothing less than making a parcel of two books to send to you. One is Desmond [MacCarthy's] last vol, *Experience* . . .

The other is the novel of Edith Wharton's in which she masticated and served up ——. "Churley" is the name she gives him, and you will find that I have indexed at the end the pages on which he appears. The rest of the novel isn't worth reading; indeed, just looking at the pages distressed me sadly. She gets faintly good ideas, and treats them in a workmanlike fashion, but good God, her style, or rather her appalling lack of that quality! After reading Henry James' prefaces (which I have enjoyed to the limit of enjoyment) poor Edith's flatness really turned my stomach — and I am fond too of the lady, and she is a gracious and affectionate friend. But can one forgive such platitude of style? I really can't do it; — but still she had a marvellous cook.

On page 346 of James' book there is a sentence which I think must have been meant for her: "We may traverse acres of pretended exhibitory prose from which the touch that directly evokes or finely presents, the touch that operates for closeness and for charm, for conviction and illusion, for communication, in a word, is unsurpassably absent." I like the use of the word "*unsurpassably*."

Hugh Trevor-Roper

Smith was fascinated by colorful churchmen of the sixteenth and seventeenth centuries in England, pulpit scholars whose splendid, hours-long sermons written in the metaphysical flights of their time were greatly admired in his own less religious and less rhetorical times. William Laud (1573–1645) was an archbishop of Canterbury who was beheaded for his loyalty to Charles I. He was appreciated only long after his death, theologians admiring him for his stout conservative sermons upholding the supremacy of the Anglican church.

When a biography of him appeared in 1940 it won Smith's admiration from its first sentence: "There are certain periods in history in which, on a superficial view, the actions of men appear to have followed rules entirely different from those with which the modern world is familiar." He immediately sent a letter of congratulations to the author of the book, a twenty-six-year-old Oxford graduate named Hugh Trevor-Roper. The young scholar was pleased with the praise of so distinguished a connoisseur and responded promptly. A friendship followed that lasted until Smith's death six years later.

After serving in the Army in the Second World War, Hugh Trevor-Roper went back to Oxford to teach history and to write. He became one of England's most distinguished historians, Regius Professor of History at Oxford and author of The Last Days of Hitler (1947) *and* Men and Events (1958) *and many other books. After more than forty years at Oxford he was elevated to the peerage as Lord Dacre of Glanton, and since 1980 he has been master of Peterhouse College at Cambridge.*

In the beginning of their friendship Trevor-Roper was stationed mainly at Barnet, Hertfordshire, which was near enough to London for him to visit Smith when he had a day off duty. They also corresponded regularly, and Smith's letters show a remarkable intellectual vigor in the eighth decade of his life and they cover all the things that interested his still-active mind. Because of their variety they are scattered throughout this collection, but many of them are personal and reflect the pleasure he took in his new friend and his admiration for him as a writer.

11 St. Leonard's Terrace
July 29, 1940

TO HUGH TREVOR-ROPER

(I think I shall call you Hugh, if you will call me in return, as everyone else does, by my Christian name.) I found after you had been here the other day Rose Macaulay's[1] last novel which I am sending you by parcel post, as I think you will like the muted passion beneath the ironical attractive surface. I am also sending you — out of vanity — the French trans-

lation of *Trivia* which you very pardonably omitted to put in
your pocket.

I hope you will pay me a visit before very long and return to
me the novel when you have read it — the other books keep
as long as you like. I hope you will enjoy the Santayana. I
notice that you are inclined to defile the altars of my other
living or not long-deceased deities, Walter Pater and Proust
and Henry James and that most exquisite master of language,
Robert Bridges. Personally, I think it a part of a liberal education to have living gods on whose altars one can lay one's
wreaths. I have had a goodly company of these, beginning
with Matthew Arnold and Walt Whitman. This felicity of
worship seems to have been denied you; or you have your gods
and heroes perhaps but don't care to mention them to the
profane. I wonder if you worship what I call mud-gods, like
my friend Desmond MacCarthy and bow before the shrines of
Bernard Shaw and Belloc[2] and a tendency is growing on you
(as it is on him) to take off your hat to J. B. Priestley. . . .[3]

But I must return to my task of writing a blurb for my book
on Milton. I don't think highly of the book, so I want it to
have at least a fine flourish of a blurb.

[1] Rose Macaulay (1881–1958), novelist, poet, journalist, historian,
anthologist, broadcaster, and letter writer. Of her twenty-three novels,
the best known were *Potterism* (1920) and *Told by an Idiot* (1923).
The novel referred to here was *And No Man's Wit*. She wrote two
books of poems, six collections of essays, and four travel descriptions.
A civilized and urbanely waspish spinster, she was noted for her wit
and she was one of the people whose company Smith most enjoyed.
He sometimes called her "Saint Rose of Hinde Street," a mocking
reference to her return to her faith in her seventh decade. Her place
in London's intellectual world was described by a speaker at a memorial
service held for her: "For so many years that gallant, thin, apparently
bloodless and yet so tough, so indomitable figure has been seen at
every party, every private view, protest meeting, cruise, literary luncheon or ecclesiastical gathering that it is hard for us to believe that she
is not to be seen at her own memorial service."
[2] Hilaire Belloc (1870–1953), prolific writer of essays, novels, verse,
travel books, history, biography, and criticism.
[3] J. B. Priestley (1894–   ), author of many popular novels, the best
known of which was *The Good Companions* (1929).

* * *

[78]

TO HUGH TREVOR-ROPER

I have just rung up Rose Macaulay — she has agreed to come
to tea with me at 4:30 next Friday and I hope you can come
then too. If you cannot come, don't trouble to write — stamps
are a consideration in these impecunious days. The lady pro-
fesses herself as much a fan of yours as you are of hers. Her
eagerness to meet you gives me grave misgivings, especially as
I recall the wise advice "Never introduce your friends to each
other" given me once by a wise and worldly friend of mine.
But I am not wise, nor, I hope completely corrupted by the
world.

Our talk yesterday has started again in my head the rusty
old machine that used to grind out the aphorisms with which
I bored the unfortunate admirers of my books. The first to
come out was a hit at these kindly geese:

It grieves me when people I like like my writing; I had
hoped that they had better taste.

Here's a hit at myself I find in my note book; I wrote it in
my innocent ante-best-seller days:

There must be something rotten in a book which attracts so
many flies.

Then I also wrote:

With money-grabbers I have no quarrel; but I think poorly
of the Magi who looked up and saw the star and stayed at
home.

I have thought of an epitaph for my tomb in the Abbey:

Dying is a dirty trick.

It gave me something of the giddy feeling of a pleasant
nightmare when you repeated yesterday some of the phrases I
toiled over long ago when writing *Trivia* — writing and rewriting day after day, year after year, in the indefatigable
pursuit of an unobtainable perfection. I lived alone in the
country; it was the happiest time of a life which everyone
told me was being wasted in a foolish if not a wicked fashion.

And now to find after twenty years that some of my winged arrows have found a target; some of my delicately fabricated flies are still a temptation to fastidious fishes, — this is a felicity added to the felicity of the toil and torment of their fabrication, which is more than any mortal has a right to ask the gods to give him. I can't tell you how funny it makes me feel.

* * *

TO HUGH TREVOR-ROPER   September 1, 1942

There is some way in which you can give me help. The reputation of a sage is made by his apothegms, or sage wisecracks. A few of my sayings are already famous and one, "Eat with the rich, but go to the play with the poor who are capable of joy," has been front-paged all over America by journalists who did not, however, relish another wise-crack: "People who write for money don't write for me."

But, of course, the output must be continuous if the sage is to keep himself before the public. I have recently been quoted as saying:

What is life without a grievance?
The truth may be defined as that which no one will, or can possibly believe.
A mingling of malice and affection can be the basis of a friendship that will outlive all other ties.
Free, opulent, fashionable, unworldly and foul-mouthed spinsters make the kindest of one's life-long friends.

* * *

11 St. Leonard's Terrace

TO HUGH TREVOR-ROPER   January 21, 1943

There is a prize to be given in the *New Statesman* for six aphorisms on England. I have furbished up a few and perhaps you will let me know which of the enclosed you pass, or send me any suggested improvements. If I win the prize money of 4 Pounds we will spend it together:

[80]

Aphorisms on England
by
An American Refugee

1 If Shakespeare is dust, there is English dust that is Shakespeare.

2 In a world stifling with uplift and national boasting, the air of England is the only air that a free spirit can breathe without choking.

3 High society is the best society in England, where, over dark growths, the sunshine on the tree tops is lovely.

4 The day before he became British, "Tomorrow," I warned Henry James, "you will want to tell lavatory stories." "But I don't know any," cried the old deracinated prestidigitator, as in despair he raised his hands to Heaven.

5 Poor old England, with her rummy National Anthem and her national heroes, Shakespeare, Nelson, and Gordon, whose statues she has to whitewash once a year.

6 Anyone in search for the home of unspotted purity would not waste much time in visiting the best public schools of England.

7 Bread sauce, cold shape and custard, the English Sunday, English clean fun and God (if he can) save England.

8 Englishmen who wear the wrong hats end in the police-courts or the gutter.

9 "Don't do what I do, but do what I tell you," the austerity propagandists bellow.

10 Our forefathers sailed to the West to find freedom; we sail back to find it in England.

* * *

11 St. Leonard's Terrace
TO HUGH TREVOR-ROPER   January 31, 1943

I have no grudge against you for not helping me, as you promised, to polish my Anglophobic aphorisms (you can't have read them or you would have seen their "down-with-England" tendency) since an Eton and Christ Church swan sailed down the Thames and spent a day helping me give them the last touches and added a couple of his own, for which he only charged me 6 Pence each. So, off they went to the *New States-man* and if they take them and pay me 4 Pounds as promised, I shall have the laugh on you and you won't get any rake-off.

* * *

TO HUGH TREVOR-ROPER

11 St. Leonard's Terrace
February 5, 1943

If you will look in the current *New Statesman* you will see before you the feast at which you will have to eat your own words. I'm sorry for you, but there it is, and the prize money will be spent in revels with my new boy-friend, to which you will not be invited. However, I am magnanimous and if envy doesn't prevent you from darkening my doors again, I will give you, as I promised, a pot of Hymettian honey which will be all the more to your taste because there is a drop of gall for me infused in its sweetness.

* * *

TO HUGH TREVOR-ROPER

11 St. Leonard's Terrace
October 6, 1940

I have just re-read Dame Una's *Laird of Abbotsford*[1] in which she describes how they tried in vain to get Sir Walter Scott to lay down his pen owing to traces of senility in his writing. As he was then eighteen years younger than I am now, I feel that I have every right to dodder. This book, by the way, I find really charming, and very good reading. Would you like me to send it to you? You would at least admire the punctuation, which, as I remember, is all my own. Dame Una used to send all her manuscripts for me to punctuate and rewrite where needed.

Beware of women, Hugh, they always have a manuscript hidden on their persons, which they pop out at you and ask you to rewrite and find a publisher for. I have learned to avoid being alone in a room with one of that dangerous sex. To act the part of Joseph is a shameful thing.

¹ Dame Una Pope-Hennessy (1876–1949) was a close friend of Smith's. She wrote biographies of Charles Dickens, Edgar Allan Poe, and Charles Kingsley, as well as the one referred to here. She was the mother of James Pope-Hennessy, also a writer and referred to in these letters, and of Sir John Pope-Hennessy, successively director of both the Victoria and Albert Museum and the British Museum in London, who is now chairman of the department of European paintings at the Metropolitan Museum of Art.

* * *

11 St. Leonard's Terrace

TO HUGH TREVOR-ROPER   April 13, 1941

In looking at the showy bookplate which adds a glory to so many of my books, I see that you have taken *Spes Mea in Deo* as your motto. Do, for Heaven's sake, drop it or you will certainly lose the war.

In my assiduous reading of Debrett [*The Peerage of England*] I have now reached Page 2318, which is not only enlightened by your name, but also by that of an ancestor of yours, happily baptized as Henry Welladvice Blayney. If Blayney is a misprint (as I hope it is) for Blarney I should like the loan of these two names from your pedigree. That Blarney suits me, all my friends would enthusiastically agree; and they would consider Welladvice as not inappropriate. Have you, by the way, many girl friends? I have just been making out a list of mine. I count among them eight wives, widows or daughters of baronets; and though a snob, there are five wives or widows of mere Knights, like Lady Raleigh and Lady Maclagan, and even four untitled spinsters. We have all grown rich and old together; the proof of our friendship is that when we meet we embrace and kiss each other.

As to *Welladvice*, evidence of my right to that name will be found in my maxims. If more proof is needed, I can add this morning's reflections:

[83]

"Live for seventy years in laziness and you will find that the best of life begins about eighty."

"If in your intriguing for power, a moral glow makes you feel that you are working for others, you may be sure that to others the glow seems reflected from the flame in which you will finally singe your wings and perish."

*　*　*

11 St. Leonard's Terrace
TO HUGH TREVOR-ROPER　　　　　September 11, 1944

I am now sending you Somerset Maugham's latest novel [*The Razor's Edge*] hoping that it will amuse you, as it amused me, to read it . . . I must say that the book's worldliness and cynicism (being qualities I like) amused me. His worldlings form a sort of Sargent gallery of accomplished portraits. I'm not a great lover of Sargent and his second-rate world of fashion, though I have, as you know, a weakness for it, but I can admire anything well done in this world of dull incompetence. Maugham can't do a saint, of course, and all the Yogi part is boring. The figure of the world-renouncer who haunts his mind is a kind of abortion — the misbegotten figure of his own conscience reproaching him always for having sold his soul — the real artist in him — for social and financial success.

I do hope your operation has gone and will go happily. If you are in for convalescence and want more books to read do let me know, and I will send you a packet if you like. I enclose a list that might amuse you; put a tick to any you would like. First on my list I put the second volume of *Gil Blas*. I think you rather failed — as indeed I did when I read it twenty years ago, in your perusal of this masterpiece. I find that Sainte-Beuve, and indeed all the best French critics (and they are of course the best critics in the world) agree that Lesage [author of *Gil Blas*] is like La Bruyère[1] an exquisite master of the best and purest and most Attic prose; and in the autobiography of the wisest of my contemporaries, the best of living critics, Santayana, I find that he says [in *Persons and Places*] that of possible Spanish ancestors he would like to imagine that the blood of Gil Blas ran in his veins. "I feel," he says, "a natural sympathy with unprejudiced minds, or, if you like, with rogues. The picaresque world is the real world and if lying and thieving and trickery are contemptible it is because the game is not worth the candle, not because the method is unworthy of the prize."

Life after all *is* a picaresque adventure and should be heartily enjoyed as such. To try to fit it into a moral design of conduct built of enduring elements, is to let oneself in for grotesque disappointment. If I were writing a Vision of Judgment, my deity would be (as Jehovah really was) a disreputable old *pícaro* but with more good nature however than the god of Israel. God's display of his backward part to Moses on the Mount shows his sense of fun. I have just read, in Carlyle's *Frederick*, Voltaire's verses to that chaste monarch congratulating him on the view of the Austrian generals who turned their backs on him and fled after his victory at Rossbach.

The List of Books

Gil Blas (Vol. 2)

Courts and Cabinets by George Peabody Gooch. Memoirs of early French and German writers. An admirable account of court memoirs.

L'Abbé Trigrane by Ferdinand Fabre. (The classic book about a great prelate.)

Travel Books

Monasteries of the Levant by Robert Curzon. [Lord Zouche, 1810–1873, a diplomat who travelled extensively in the Levant.]

The Bible in Spain by George Borrow.

Malay Archipelago by [Alfred Russel] Wallace [1823–1913].

Travels on the Amazon by Wallace.

The Naturalist in Nicaragua by [Thomas] Belt [1832–1878].

In an Enchanted Island: Cyprus by [William H.] Mallock [1849–1923].

Pearl Diver: Adventuring Over and Under the South Seas by [Victor] Berge [and Henry W. Lanier]. One of the most fascinating books I have ever read.

[1] Jean de La Bruyère (1645–1696), French author of social satire and maxims.

* * *

11 St. Leonard's Terrace
                                           September 28, 1944

I have been wondering whether I have not incurred your dis-
favor by the last parcel of books I sent you. Though you had
put into my hands the key to the chamber of the horrors of
your taste by quoting to me the saying (which Walter Scott
was fond of) that "scornful dogs will eat dirty puddings," I
nevertheless posted off to you two rice or suet puddings from
the kitchen of the Whigs. I now fear that if you unwisely
read them, you will find them too vapid and insipid even for
your uncorrupted mind. To remedy this and to appease you
(and that I may one day appease you is a vain fond hope of
mine, faced as I feel myself to be — with the horror of your
implacable disapproval) I am sending herewith three un-
edifying volumes. One is a defense of T. S. Eliot against the
attacks rudely made by the constipationists on his achievement
and output. The others are two more volumes of the un-
consecrated author of *The Razor's Edge,* which I was so glad
you liked. In *Cakes and Ale* you will find the red-hot poker
that killed Hugh Walpole and the best of those honest whores
Maugham presents so well. Driffield (Thomas Hardy, of
course) is another abortion-birth of Willy Maugham's own
conscience. The second Mrs. Driffield is a photo straight from
life. Shortly after the book was published I sat by a "Mrs.
Thomas Hardy" at a luncheon party in Lady Noble's palace
and this female's talk about social life in Dorsetshire seemed
to come so directly word for word out of *Cakes and Ale* that I
honestly believe that she was a sham Mrs. Hardy acting the
part for fun.

The other volume is a collection of Maugham's short
stories. To read them all will more than sate you; but "The
Alien Corn" I think the best short story of this century; and
some of the others, which I have marked, are good. But when
(as Henry James would have put it) I say they are "good," I
mean that they are "bad," for they are all, or almost all, hor-
ribly true stories — ghastly betrayals of confidences the publication of which has ruined the lives of the hosts who kindly

entertained him in the East and confided in him the sad secrets of their frustrated lives. The decent person I am at heart — as decent, Willy Maugham would say, as Hugh Walpole — gets rather disenchanted by too many of these masterpieces of disloyalty and betrayal; and I hope you share my distaste.

Places and Pleasures

How often my soul visits the National Gallery,
and how seldom I go there myself.

— Afterthoughts

Smith was a much-traveled man and felt at home in many
places: London always fascinated him and he seldom left there
in his later years; Paris and Venice were cities of glamour to
him when he was young; Florence, a familiar joy when he
stayed there frequently with the Berensons. He loved ships
and sailing and went on modest cruises in the English coastal
waters and on elaborate cruises in the Mediterranean, such as
the one he describes here. He once wrote that the main reason
he liked having money was that it enabled him to travel in
comfort; obviously he did that.

*   *   *

Paris

15 Rue du Sommerard, Paris

TO BERTRAND RUSSELL   October 25, 1891

I have been meaning to write to you before, to tell you how
much I enjoyed my visit to Cambridge, but I have been
through such a season of woe in settling myself here! It is all
due to that bothersome new order, for it is very hard to get
rooms within the fixed margin, and I am much too proud to
confess an excess so soon. So I have at last settled myself in
the Latin Quarter, up seven flights of stairs, and I find that the
spiritual pride that fills my breast more than amply compen-

sates for all the bother. It *is* nice to feel better than one's neighbors! I met a friend yesterday who is living in cushioned ease across the river, and I felt so very superior. I am rather afraid that when I write to my adviser, I shall receive a hair shirt by return of post. Have you tried to observe the discipline? I do not speak evil, for I have no one to speak it to, though I think it of my landlady. And the other day, I was so reduced by the state of my things when I moved here that I could do nothing but eat a bun and read Tid-bits.

I have begun to write a novel, but be assured, it is not religious, and is not to be rejected by publishers for a year or two yet.

My journey here after I left you was most amusing. On the steamer we sat in rows and glared at each other, after the pleasant English manner. There was a young married couple who stood out as a warning and a lesson to youth. He was a puzzled looking, beardless young man, and she was a limp figure of a woman, and there was a baby. The husband poured his wife into an arm chair, and then walked up and down with the baby. Then he stood for a long while, looking at the watery horizon as if he were asking some question of it. But the dismal unwellness of his wife and baby soon put an end to his meditations. What a warning to youth! And I might have been in his place!

* * *

15 Rue du Sommerard, Paris
TO BERTRAND RUSSELL   December 3, 1891

I live here alone with the greatest contentment. One inherits, when one comes here, such a wealth of tradition and civilization! The achievements of three or four centuries of intelligence and taste — that is what one has at Paris. I was bewildered at first, and shivered on the brink, and was homesick for England, but now I have come to love Paris perfectly.

Do write again when you have collected more sins, and tell me whether the fear of penance acts on you in the cause of virtue. It does on a cowardly nature like mine.

* * *

[89]

TO BERTRAND RUSSELL   January 11, 1892

I am living in great quiet and contentment. A certain portion of the day I devote to enriching the English language with rules and moralities, the rest of the time I contemplate the mind of man as expressed in art and literature. I am thirsting of course for that moment — and without doubt the moment will come — when I shall hear my name sounded by all Fame's tongues and trumpets, and see it misspelled in all the newspapers. But I content myself in the meantime, by posing as a poet in the drawing rooms of credulous American ladies.

As a novelist or "fictionist" to use the Star expression, I make it my aim to show up in my tales, in which truth is artistically mingled with morality, "Cupid and all his wanton snares." I also wish to illustrate some of the incidents of the eternal war between the sexes. What will the whited sepulchres of America say? *Je m'en fiche.*

Well, it is pleasant thus to expatiate upon my own precious identity.

I suppose you are "on the threshold" — as one says, when one wishes to write high style — the threshold of another term — and so resuming my character of moral adviser I will salt this letter with some sententious phrase, if I can find one that is both true and fresh — but I cannot think of any — the truth is always so banal — that is why the paradox has such a pull over it.

*   *   *

14 Rue de la Grande Chaumière
TO BERTRAND RUSSELL   March 19, 1892

As you see by my address, I have moved again, and I am at last settled in a little apartment furnished by myself. I am in Bohemia, a most charming country inhabited entirely by French Watchmen and American and English art students, young men and women, who live in simple elegance and *déshabille.* My two Pounds a week seems almost gross extravagance here, and one's eyes are never wounded by the sight of clean linen and new coats. Really you can't imagine how charming it is here — everybody young, poor and intelligent and hard at work.

When I came here first, I knew some "society" people on the other side of the river, and used to go and take tea and talk platitudes with them, but now their lives seem so empty, their minds so waste and void of sense, that I cannot approach them without a headache of boredom. How dull and unintelligent people can make themselves if they but try.

* * *

14 Rue de la Grande Chaumière
TO BERTRAND RUSSELL   February 14, 1893

Paris welcomed me as all her own, when I got here and I have been living in the charm of this delightful and terrible place. For it is pretty terrible in many ways, at least the part of Paris I live in. Perhaps it is the wickedness of Paris itself, perhaps the fact that people live in this quarter without conventions or disguises or perhaps — which I am inclined to believe — the life of artists is almost always tragical — or not wanting at least in elements of Tragedy — that gives me the sense of the wretchedness and the fineness of life here. Just think, this very morning I discovered that a girl here I know had gone mad. She came in to see me, begged me to help her write a book to attack French immorality and now I am waiting to see the doctor I sent for, to see if we must shut her up.

As for "morality" well — one finds plenty of the other thing, both in women and men. I met the other day one of the Young Davies' at Studd's studio — and my heart sank a little at the sight of another nice young Englishman come to live in Paris. But he I suppose can take care of himself.

But I must not abuse Paris too much, for after all this, and perhaps on account of it, Paris is beyond measure interesting. There are big stakes to be won or lost and everybody is playing for them.

Venice

I am living like a Prince here in Venice. I am already trans-
ported — how does Plato put it — into the Islands of the
Blest. Imagine a great garden, walled in from the Grand Canal
by the wings of a great unfinished palace. One of the wings I
have to myself — I have bought a little boat which is anchored
just under my windows. From across the garden good dinners
and breakfasts are brought to me. After breakfast I take a little
turn in my boat; then I spend the morning reading letters
praising my book [*The Youth of Parnassus*] or planning other
books with nice blue covers, and all the afternoons I float over
the great gray windless lagoons, visiting little islands where
there is a Gothic church, perhaps a town or an early basilica.
In the other wing of the palace there lives a pleasant Magdalen
undergraduate who is supposed to be reading history, but who
really lives in my boat all day long. Every evening we are out
for hours either following the florid sentimental music, as it
splashes up the Grand Canal, or pushing our way at random
through the little black canals — so black and deep at night,
between the enormous palaces that they seem almost like sub-
terranean rivers. But suddenly we come on a lighted square
noisy with feet and music — then lunge again into the silence
and blackness.

Windsor

19 Sheep Street, Windsor

Thee can imagine how I have enjoyed Windsor; how I have
mused, wandered, sailed, bathed, prayed in St. George's
chapel, sat and read on the terrace, elegized and wandered
about Eton — what a home for the soul, what a place to be
melancholy in! The castle rising white in the twilight, or
gilded by the late sun, flashes with a kindly beauty that amazes
me. I love the little walled-in cathedral town, with the little
red houses and gray chapel, where they chant prayers and
psalms like spells — marvellous words, incantations, which

forever chanted, will make England forever great. "No, not when thou hast smitten us unto the place of the Dragons, and covered us with the shadow of death," they sang yesterday. "The King's daughter is all glorious within, her clothing is of wrought gold, she shall be brought unto the King in raiment of needle work, the Virgins that be her fellows shall bear her company." It's words like these, chanted by boys, and by old canonical warlocks and wizards that make England rule the seas!

A Cruise with Edith Wharton

In the spring of 1926 with the profits from a novel called The Mother's Recompense, Mrs. Wharton chartered a 360-ton steam yacht, the Osprey, and invited the Berensons to go on a cruise in the Mediterranean and Aegean seas. They declined, citing their fear of travel by water, but suggested that she ask Smith in their place. The trip lasted ten weeks.

I Tatti, Florence

TO EDITH WHARTON   February 2, 1926

Thank you very much for your note and most kind invitation. Of course I accept with the wildest alacrity. Two of the things I love best, the sea and Greece, and then the prospects of such good company too. I will come to Hyères, as you suggest, on March 31 and if I can spend April on the yacht, I shall be very happy. I have promised to join the B.B.'s — that craven and cowardly couple — in Constantinople at the beginning of May. In the meantime, I shall make them sup on tales of maritime disaster, lest an unhappy impulse should seize them to pre-occupy my dreamed of cabin.

* * *

I Tatti

TO KENNETH CLARK   February 1926

I am much looking forward to my Aegean cruise, though I feel that there is something shocking in visiting those shrines of immortality on the profits of an ephemeral best-seller of a year, for it is Mrs. Wharton's latest novel which is to pay the charter of the *Osprey*. As to the *Osprey* herself, I dare say I shall find her magnificent. I have never been on a steam yacht, so have no ideals or standards connected with them. My own little yawl was simplicity itself, and Sir Hubert Parry's ketch in which we used to bang into the teeth of the blackest storms, was hardly more luxurious. One of my proudest memories is coming out to eat a good breakfast one morning when most of the crew was sea-sick and the "governor" himself was kept in his bunk by what he euphemistically called a headache. But I was more an ignorant than an intrepid sailor and I find in Walter Raleigh's letters the following cruel but true sentence, written when cruising with him, "P.S. [Pearsall Smith] is anxious to be a sea-dog but I tell him he won't get beyond being a waterside character — if so far." I can only reply to that beloved ghost that he himself was not even a waterside character — but those retorts alas are vain.

* * *

Saint-Claire du Château, Hyères, France

TO HIS SISTER MARY   March 30, 1926

Our company is assembled, the yacht is anchored in the sea below, and we embark this afternoon,

> A ship is floating in the harbor now,
> A breeze is fluttering on the mountain brow,
> There is a path on the sea's azure floor

etc etc but fortunately there is no Emily to embark with, only a party of elderly worldlings, who will be, I hope, easier to get on with. It *seems* like a delightful adventure, and will, I hope, be so. Little dim pictures of old harbors and islands rise now and then before my imagination, to vanish and be driven away by thoughts about socks and underclothes. These anticipations will fill themselves out with great richness, but they are in a way one of the most delicate pleasures of travelling.

* * *

TO HIS SISTER MARY

The yacht is deliciously comfortable . . . the company is very pleasant. Mrs. Wharton is always amusing and is really most considerate except when her rage for picture post-cards comes upon her and then everything has to pause until it is satisfied. She reminds me of Carey [Thomas] with her passion for buying spoons and paperweights in every city. It is really plucky for Mrs. Wharton to take this trip as any roll of the yacht makes her sea-sick and she has had to spend two or three days in bed already. The rest of us are good sailors and haven't been upset at all. Norton[1] is pleasant company, Lawrence harmless and insignificant, Mrs. Chanler [whose reminiscences, *Autumn in the Valley,* he was to enjoy ten years later] twitters amiably away, almost always on a subject quite different from the subject of the rest of the conversation. [The guests] are delightfully easy to get on with, elderly, amused, enthusiastic worldlings, fond of poetry and sight-seeing, though their motto is that of the old lady in one of Mrs. Wharton's anecdotes, who always said, "An hour is enough of anything."

The charter of the yacht costs over 1,000 Pounds a month and with the food and fuel must be pretty big.

[1] Robert Norton was a young Englishman, a product of Eton and Cambridge, who was a member of Mrs. Wharton's social circle. He was a painter and poet and did some verse translations.

* * *

TO HIS SISTER ALYS

Mrs. Wharton is like Carey [Thomas] in many ways, only she can't make, like Carey, the weather. She was very angry today because the sea was rough and we had to change our anchorage. "The sea simply must be calm," she said, "as I simply have to be in Athens at 10." She is very jolly and full of fun, and really very kind, though her shyness often makes her seem rude and insolent.

* * *

[95]

On board the *Osprey*

May 4, 1926

We had to go back from Chalchis to Athens to take on
more oil; it is difficult to get oil in these ports, and the yacht
only carries enough for a certain distance; however, it is a
great relief to have everything clean — no smoke, and none of
the dirt of coaling up. From Athens we went to Delos, a bleak
impressive little island, a sort of ghostly city of ruins and
marble fragments but nothing of great artistic value. The next
night we anchored at Patmos, and rode up to its ancient
fortress-monastery, which is very ancient and picturesque. The
next days to me are rather dim, as my attention was turned on
my insides rather than the outward world. I had in fact a
severe and disgusting attack of bowel trouble, which kept me
in bed two days and from which I am only just recovering. A
great nuisance, but the sort of thing that happens in these
climates, and I feel really all right this morning, only a little
weak. Mrs. Wharton's maid Elise is an excellent doctor, and
looked after me with great kindness. The yacht in the meantime was cruising among the Dodecanese, with their romantic
mountains, deep harbors, and little white semi-Oriental mountain towns and old monasteries, but I only caught glimpses of
these through my porthole, and that of the W.C. — a most
inadequate, but I believe not uncommon way of seeing the
East. At each place the party went ashore, taking sometimes
long rides on mules over the mountains — the two old ladies
have a wonderful spirit and are passionate sight-seers, though
Mrs. Wharton soon drains the cup of aesthetic sensation.

The yacht is so very comfortable, and the service so perfect,
that one gets unfitted for the ordinary incidents of travel, such
as hotels and railway trains, etc. I don't know how I shall get
unmillionaired again.

*   *   *

TO KENNETH CLARK

Here I am in the *Osprey* anchored off the coast of Attica with the Parthenon shining in the distance. We left the Riviera two weeks ago, stopped at Palermo, cruised among the Ionian isles, visited Olympia and Delphi and now mean to spend a week seeing the sights of Athens. Then we sail for the Aegean islands, Crete, and Cyprus, then back via Athens to Marseilles. It is all extremely pleasant, and the *Osprey* seems to us all that we could desire, and some of our company are used to lordly yachting. Our captain and crew are all Scotch, and mostly seem to come from Paisley — we are a little afraid of them, to tell the truth, and want to assert ourselves, but don't quite yet know how to do it. The captain will anchor away off from shore and there is a motor launch we long to use, but there seem to be mysterious reasons why it should never touch the water. We began by letting ourselves be rowed ashore in shore boats, which was a mistake, as I told Mrs. Wharton; I urged her to establish her prestige, but the Scotch inspire her with fear. Otherwise, they are all we could wish, except their extreme reserve makes it difficult to establish any human relations with them. But perhaps this reserve will thaw as the cruise proceeds.

We are a party of five elderly, disillusioned, polite and amused worldlings, pleased to be old and rich and full of curiosity, and fond of sight-seeing, and Mrs. Wharton planned this trip as a "sunset cruise" before our old bones can no longer be taken travelling. We are enjoying it immensely and only wish that we had known in youth that age could bring with it such golden pleasures — take it from me that the best of life is after fifty. But you won't believe it.

Mansfield Park

Mansfield Park *was Smith's favorite among Jane Austen's books. He was, therefore, particularly interested when a specific place was identified as the actual setting of the novel. It*

[97]

was Cottesbrooke Hall, nine miles north of Northampton.
When the estate came onto the market in 1935 Smith visited
it and wrote of his experience in a letter to Dr. Robert W.
Chapman, editor of the Collected Works of Jane Austen.

London
TO DR. ROBERT W. CHAPMAN   June 14, 1935

I do wish you could have joined us at Mansfield Park; the day
was filled to the brim with literary interest — and psycho-
logical as well. I procured an order to view the house and got
my neighbor, Sir Trevor Bigham and his wife to motor me
down there. All went well at first; Bigham indeed refused to
let me stop and shed a tear on the tomb of Mrs. Humphrey
Ward ("Mary," as I suppose you would call her) as he said
that was silly, and he took but a tepid interest in the kennels
of the Pytchley hounds at Brixworth two miles from Mansfield Park. But he became more and more worried as we proceeded about the attitude we should adopt at Mansfield if we
found its owner, Captain Brassey, in residence and had to
account to him for our visitation. Any reference to the novel,
he felt, would be out of place and would almost certainly not
be understood. All that, I told him to leave to me — he was a
man of the world, a K.B.E., a son of a peer of the realm, as
well as a high official of Scotland Yard and I felt perfect con-
fidence that he could carry off the situation. "Why not," I
suggested, "say that you are giving up your house at Dorking
because you want a place where there is better hunting? Or
why not pretend that you have come from Scotland Yard to
investigate some crime? Or, if you like, I will impersonate a
millionaire and say that the house is pretty enough but too
small after all for my purposes especially as there was only
stabling for seventeen horses."

"But all that would be deception," he protested.

"But surely you must practice a lot of deception at Scotland
Yard," I answered.

"I don't," he answered. "I leave that to others" and then he
fell into dark musing, the result of which was his decision that
he would say he was only visiting the place in passing, to

advise a friend who thought of purchasing it for himself. I told him that this was rather funking the dilemma; but with great tact I didn't add that this seemed just as much a pretense as the others.

We visited the charming village, the church with the monuments of Sir Thomas and Lady Bertram, of the Grants and Mrs. Norris and of Julia (there is none of course to Maria) and the big rectory, Dr. Grant's field (which had horses in it) and Mrs. Norris' cottage, and then went to eat the luncheon we had brought with us to the park. I insisted on sitting at my ease on the grass; my companion didn't at all like this liberty and when the time came to visit the house he declared that he wouldn't go until he met the family, that he would feel himself an impostor, which would make him too uncomfortable. He would wait for me however with his wife in the car and he finally agreed that if I found that the family was away and only the butler (to whom we should give a handsome tip) was to show us around, he would come if I waved my handkerchief. So, I walked up to the splendid entrance, showed my order to view and when I was told the family was away, I waved to the Bighams in the distance (they wouldn't let their car approach the house) and they joined me. We saw it all — the library and the billiard room, the stairs on which Fanny wept, her rest room with its empty fire grate and every detail described so accurately in the novel. (Jane Austen must certainly have been there — I will take my oath on that.)

For my companion's attack of proper feelings several explanations have suggested themselves:

1. They were the feelings of an English gentleman to which I can make no pretensions, not being an Englishman, and not I daresay a gentleman in the accepted sense.

2. Sir Trevor felt that his soft hat wasn't quite the thing. I wore a bowler as I felt that that was more correct.

3. An unconscious fear (unknown to himself, but capable of psychoanalysis) of meeting Sir Thomas Bertram, which would have been, of course, appalling. Indeed, there was a dreadful moment when we stood in his library, and felt that Julia might suddenly burst in to exclaim "My father is come! He is in the hall at this moment."

The Social Life

How awful to reflect that what people say of us
is true.

— Afterthoughts

English Country Swells

Hotel des Indes, The Hague

TO HIS SISTER MARY September 12, 1885

We arrived here this afternoon from Broadlands,[1] which we
left yesterday. We had a very pleasant visit and stayed longer
than we expected. There were a number of people staying
there, swells apparently of different degree. Some were interesting — some weren't in themselves, but they all were
worth study as types. I like once in a while to get among people with decided views of their own about themselves and the
world in general and with nice clean-cut prejudices — they
seem like hard-boiled eggs, not that they have ever been hard-
boiled, they were just born so and their parents were hard-
boiled before them. They seemed so certain that their way was
right — that the answer to the riddle of the ages was *their*
comfortable houses and hunting and afternoon tea and for the
poor people, O somebody to patronize them and somebody to
look up to — I should like to give them all a little dose of the
French Revolution just to shake them up.

[1] Broadlands in Hampshire was the country seat of Lord and Lady
Mount Temple, friends of Smith's family. Theirs was a world, he
wrote in *Unforgotten Years*, of "large, opulent, ruddy aristocrats of
great wealth and high position." It was at Broadlands that the future
Queen Elizabeth II of England spent her honeymoon in 1947.

The New Parson

TO HIS MOTHER   Haslemere, 1892

The great excitement here is the new parson, who comes next
month. Mrs. Duke is going to ask him to lunch, but she cannot decide what to have, and every day she and the doctor
discuss it. The doctor wants her to do it in the grand style,
with salmon and green peas, and I have suggested a pig's head
as a compromise. We know nothing about the man except that
Mrs. Salvin doesn't like him — which we think a good sign.

A Country Scene

*Sir William Rothenstein (1872–1945) was a British artist,
perhaps known for his portrait drawings. He wrote a three-
volume autobiography,* Men and Memories *(1931).*

                                              Haslemere
TO WILLIAM ROTHENSTEIN   August 18, 1893

I got back here a day or two ago, after a delightful visit. It was
a charming and shabby old park, with a quaint ugly house and
as soon as I arrived I felt myself back in 1830. A footman ran
out across the lawn to let my trap in, and Lady Jane received
me, and we walked out in the first twilight, onto a long and
ancient terrace, with over-arching elms down the green perspective of which I saw advancing several maidens and young
men. There were flower baskets and little woolly dogs — and
of course I saw at once that they were walking out of the
English novel to welcome me. Indeed the whole time I was
between the covers of the old-fashioned novel: in the still hot
afternoons I would sit talking to Lady Jane; a little way off the
Squire was surveying his acres and whistling to his dogs, while
from the river that lapped away below the terrace there came
echoes of talk and laughter and then we would see a boat
splashing up slowly, in which a young lady in pink was being
rowed by a charming young man in white. Their talk was
about the Prince Consort, I make sure, and Landseer's wonderful pictures of animals and Canova's sculpture, which he said
was what we must admire. But Lady Jane and I were more

serious; fixing her eye on the horizon, she told me of the deplorable changes that were coming over the countryside; old families gone away, their places taken by dreadful *nouveaux riches;* the peasantry losing their reverence for the squires; the farmers aping gentlemen, and even maids in the best houses wearing hats with flowers in them instead of bonnets. Lady Jane was short and thin and strenuous, she has a fine, even aristocratic profile and always wore a creaking silk dress with a train. We found that we had many sympathies in common and we both deplored the dreadful spread of Atheism and Socialism and all their evil consequences; old places ceasing to be kept up as they used to be; men of place and position marrying Americans, of whose antecedents Heaven only knows what they are.

Then we agreed too about the horrid tone of modern French literature, which, as we put it, always left a bad taste in the mouth — and as for their pictures, well, it was hardly decent so much as to mention them. Poor Lady Jane! She showed me her needle work, and a polar bear on an iceberg — that she had painted on a screen.

Oscar Wilde

TO ROBERT C. TREVELYAN   1898

I don't suppose you or Roger [Fry] are likely to see anything of Oscar Wilde, who is at Posillipo. Mrs. Costelloe has rather melancholy accounts of him. He is surrounded by the old low lot, makes money by writing obscenities for Smithers, and though he would like to pull himself together, he feels that it is no use, as all decent people have abandoned him. Someone who has just seen him implored Mrs. Costelloe to get his former friends to write to him — so if you see any of them tell them. Villa Giudice, Posillipo, is his address. Sebastian Melmoth he calls himself.

A Smug Young Man

TO HIS SISTER ALYS

Trevy [Robert C. Trevelyan] is here, mild and quite pleasant.
There is also here a cousin of B.B.'s — a mild smug young
man in spectacles, quite harmless, and inconceivably stupid —
and by the irony of God, a student of aesthetics. For two days
he was quite quiet, and we thought overcome by B.B.'s knowledge, and all our brilliancy; however, I had my suspicions, so
yesterday, when he was driving down with Mary and myself,
I began to draw him [out] and found that he considers himself
a much more profound thinker than any of us — B.B.'s work
is in his opinion all very well as far as it goes, only *he* means
to go *much* further; starting from the point of view of taking
all life and thought as his subject, he has already studied meta-
physics, ethics, and physics and has qualified himself for
aesthetics by playing on the violin, and writing poetry, and he
means to study painting 4 months to get the atmosphere and
qualify himself for that art, as of course only an artist is capable of criticizing art. Last night we drew him [out] on music
— had he a theory of music? He only had the foundations and
outlines of one he said modestly, and then he went on to
expound it while we all quaked with suppressed laughter . . .
But really I can give no conceivable idea of the fatuousness
and woolly absurdity of his ideas. They are like a collection of
all the old hats of ten and fifteen years ago.

A Garden Party

TO HIS SISTER ALYS

The Kinsellas[1] seem to be enjoying themselves very much . . .
Miss Louise finds the English very sober and staid, she admires
them, thinks them good and nice but chafes a little at their
self-control. "Do they never have moments of expansion?",
she asked me. Certainly they do not at garden parties. We
went to a party on Saturday — there were four men in top
hats and long black coats, who stood and sang solemnly by a

flower bed of dark purple pansies, a semi-circle of people stood on the other side, with faces of incurable melancholy — it was exactly like an interment!

Then we went to some amateur theatricals, which were very funny and unreal, but the audience were very good. When a youthful undergraduate waved his arms and exclaimed "I must be calm, I must control myself," they took him at his word and gave most generous sympathy to his state of uncontrollable excitement.

1 Three American young women who were friends of Smith's family.

A Breach-of-Promise Suit

Villa Rosa, Fiesole

TO HIS MOTHER   November 4, 1900

Today is a lovely day of sunshine. We are expecting to lunch a Miss C . . . [illegible]. Her brother, a quaint, formal young man, lives in Florence. He had a breach of promise case in England, had to pay 1,000 Pounds to the young lady, whom he found to be quite unsuitable after he got engaged, and so as he tells everybody he does not care, being a sensitive person, to return to England. It seems to me that a sensitive person would say nothing of an adventure of that kind! However he tells you all the details, and his special grievance seems to be that she accepted the money, and only valued his affections at 1,000 Pounds. "She ought to have taken nothing, or a very large sum," he says. Queer world.

The New King

Oxford

TO HIS SISTER ALYS   January 24, 1901

I enclose a picture of the new King [Edward VII] for Bertie. I feel myself in the 18th century with a King, and all the court ceremonies. I rather like the idea of a foolish fat King — it seems so English somehow, and how charming if one can see his great fat high-rouged hideous mistresses driving around London in splendid gilt coaches with 6 horses! I shall wear a powdered wig and tell funny stories about the Duke of Newcastle!

Praise

Haslemere
TO HELEN THOMAS FLEXNER   July 3, 1901

Fernhurst is all as you know it — my house and garden are prettier than ever and the taste for showing it off grows on me. I shall end like Shenstone[1] whom Dr. Johnson describes hopping along his garden walls and who "only enjoyed his house when people of note came to see and commend it."

[1] William Shenstone (1714–1763), a pastoral poet.

Peace and Quiet

London
TO HIS MOTHER   September 3, 1901

Percy[1] dined here last night. Today he is going to stay with Miss Ethel Smyth[2] who is to take him to call on the Empress Eugénie. He is pleased but frightened at the thought of meeting royalty. He told me that he not only suffers from the memory of *faux pas* he has made but even from imaginary ones — he thinks of awful things he might have said or done and then suffers agonies of remorse. Another thing amused me: he has been staying with his brother-in-law's family in Norfolk — the mother is a fierce — scolding — fussing person, and the father wishes only for peace and quiet. He wanders about silently in felt slippers and talks, when he talks at all, in a low voice. One evening after dinner he got up suddenly and walked quietly out of the room, somewhat to the family's surprise. Shortly afterwards they found that the curtains were on fire. The old gentleman had seen it and had gone away to avoid a fuss!

[1] Percy Feilding (b. 1867), a friend of Smith's, who ran an antique shop in Pimlico with Smith and Philip Morrell for a short time.
[2] Dame Ethel Smyth (1858–1944), one of the foremost English composers of her day.

Pulpit Platitudes

TO HIS SISTER ALYS   June 10, 1902

I went with the Morrells on Sunday evening to church. I
wanted to hear the new Vicar. He preached what seemed to
Philip and me a terribly pretentious and platitudinous sermon
— something perfectly appalling from the point of view of
style. "The past is behind us," with great emphasis. "The
present is with us, the future," with still more emphasis, "is
before us!" What appalling things sermons are! Philip
squirmed and twisted and wrung his hands, but dear Lady
Ottoline dozed and didn't listen. I was worn to a rag with the
agony of listening. And Dr. Duke told me that the sermon was
too intellectual and far above the congregation and that the
Vicar is much too clever a man to stay in Fernhurst. It all
suggests thoughts too deep for words.

The Morrells liked the Webbs immensely and Mrs. Webb
was very nice to Lady Ottoline. Philip and Lady Ottoline are
both radicals, and like radicals much more than Tories, in
spite of their embattled Tory families. They are very happy
and very much in love, and it does one good to see them. They
would love to have a cottage in this neighborhood and want
very much to come back.

Mrs. Webb is looking forward very much to going to
Switzerland, and I think she will be an excellent companion.

Village Morals

TO HIS SISTER ALYS   July 3, 1902

Fernhurst is deserted this week and I have seen no one but
the Vicar, whom I met yesterday in the road. He told me that
the Miss G—— I spoke to thee about who broke her arm has
had two illegitimate sons, and for this reason she was not
looked upon with a favorable eye by the guardians and church
authorities. He said this most apologetically either out of
deference to what he thought would be my views on such a
point of morals, or else to show that he was above all such

petty prejudices. But I think a clergyman ought to have more respect for the rites he administers — just as a matter of business, if for no other reason.

I have three bee-hives now in my garden and take the greatest pleasure in watching them. They are frightfully busy all day and even late at night the hives are full of the noise and hum of work. They ought to be a good example to me, or I ought to be a good example to them — it depends on one's view of the meaning of life. I think I shall get some honey and sit down in front of the hives and eat it in a leisurely manner, just to show them that one ought to enjoy life and the summer hours.

Freedom

Haslemere

TO HIS SISTER ALYS   July 2, 1903

I got a good dressing down yesterday from Mrs. Mason, an American lady who is staying at Upperfold. She lectured me at length on the duty of every man to provide for the happiness of some woman. The sight of a free man, a free American man, made her beside herself with fury. I can imagine Southerners in the time of slavery feeling like that when they saw a free Negro. I tried to explain to her that I had escaped to a free soil but she would have none of it.

Tell Bertie (apropos of our discussion on Saturday) that prose is the statement of a beautiful mind; poetry the ecstasy of it.

But prose too has its ecstasies.

An Elopement

Haslemere

TO HIS MOTHER   June 3, 1904

The great excitement in Fernhurst is still the elopement. (The woman who kept the institute has run off with one of their lodgers — quite a young man, taking all her husband's savings

— 100 Pounds.) Today there is a sale of the furniture and belongings of the deserted husband — all that the wife and the lodger left him, for they took away the linen and blankets and many other things. Imagine the woman's emotions as she drove off in V——'s trap and took her last look at Fernhurst, where she had lived twenty years, and which she would probably never see again! A great moment for a middle-aged Fernhurst woman. I think some of the others envy her, and public opinion would all be on her side if she had not taken her husband's money. He was the dullest and most boring kind of man.

The police think the couple have gone to America, and I don't suppose they will ever be caught.

The Extra Wife

Haslemere
TO HIS MOTHER   October 16, 1904

Here is another Fernhurst story: The butcher, whose father of 86 disappeared, has now gone off himself into unknown parts. It seems that he had spent some years in America and last week an American wife and two children appeared at Liphook in his pursuit. As he already had an English wife and family, he apparently decided that the best thing to do was to desert them both. In warning Ray and Karin [his nieces] against the perfidy of the male sex thee would do well to lay some stress on the special depravity of butchers.

Candida

Haslemere
TO HIS MOTHER   November 30, 1904

I enjoyed going to *Candida* very much with Ray and Karin — they are admirable critics. I think we agreed about the play — that it was very interesting and amusing but unreal somehow. Bernard Shaw's human nature isn't real human nature and although he doesn't "hit below the belt" with scenes of hackneyed emotion he leaves you empty. He creates a world of his own, but it isn't a world of beauty, but one of freaks and paradox. The idea of a fine woman loving a man because he is weak and a windbag makes a dramatic bid for a play but it's rather an unreal and impossible situation in life. As Ray remarked, how could they go on with life the next day?

A Wedding

TO HIS MOTHER

Oxford
April 27, 1905

I went to Freddie Morrell's[1] wedding today, walking through Oxford in a top hat which was a strange sensation. Fortunately, it didn't rain. There was the usual crush of people in their best clothes, the usual crowds of people about the church, and the usual service, which is really one of the most improper things I have ever heard! At weddings I am always woefully afraid that the bridegroom or the bride won't appear, and the other one be left waiting at the altar. One reads of it happening so often in novels and in the newspapers — however, both were on time, and everything went successfully. It is a most suitable if rather commonplace match, like something in a novel by Trollope and Lady Ottoline says it is not very romantic — not that they are not in love, but just because it is so suitable. But it is not the duty of people to amaze the world by their marriages. Lady Ottoline herself was sufficiently odd by her appearance to make the wedding unusual.

[1] Philip Morrell's sister Frederica.

Social Climbing

TO HIS MOTHER

Haslemere
November 5, 1905

I see there is a sign out that the Millhanger is to be let furnished. The owner Mrs. C—— (a daughter of an old Fernhurst washerwoman) came there this summer and expected to set up as a lady, and to be called on by the nobility and gentry of Fernhurst, so she cut all her old friends. The nobility and gentry, however, did not call, her humble friends now refuse her advances, so she is left entirely alone, and is going to her "town house."

Lady Queensberry

Haslemere
TO HIS MOTHER   November 8, 1905

Lady Queensberry [she was the mother of Lord Alfred Douglas, Oscar Wilde's friend] was delighted with the cottage yesterday. [It was a quaint old cottage nearby recommended by Smith.] We impressed on her the drawbacks and let her discover the merits for herself. She is a frail, vague, faded, gentle and crushed but still beautiful creature, and all the horrors she has been through — a dreadful father, a mad sister, a husband who wanted to murder her, an eldest son who shot himself, etc etc. She wanders about in thin high-heeled slippers, with a detective story in one hand and a rubber hot water bottle in the other, and apparently gets some comfort from each, though the book is always getting lost and the hot water bottle has to be refilled continually, so that her life still has its troubles.

Local Politics

Oxford
TO HIS MOTHER   January 23, 1906

As thee will probably have seen by the evening papers, Philip Morrell has won his election [as a Member of Parliament]. It has been most exciting and I am glad it is over. I went out yesterday (which was the polling day) to a little village outside Oxford and helped in bringing the voters to the polls. There was a crowd of shrill radical children ready to hoot at anyone in blue and to cheer the red color. The Tory candidate was hooted in a satisfactory manner and soon a splendid motor covered with red came along and in it Philip and Lady Ottoline looking very happy and handsome. The children set up the loudest yell I have ever heard, and all the time the motor stopped kept shrieking an election song in poor Lady Ottoline's ears, till we were all deafened. They had the same reception at every village and as they spent their day going from one to another they must have been nearly dead by evening.

This morning I went to the county hall to hear the result declared. It was a great dingy place, and there were hundreds of Liberal working-men there, each one full of cheers and yells ready to burst out at the end. There was a closed door, behind which the vote was being counted in the presence of the candidates, and outside the door were ranged on either side the respective families dressed in their proper colors and full of uncomfortable emotions. Occasionally the sacred door would open a crack, and then shut again. Finally, the high sheriff came out and mounted on some steps and as soon as he said "Morrell" there was a wild scene of excitement. The excitement grew when Philip came out and kissed Lady Ottoline, and shook hands with his supporters, and beamed smiles on everyone. He then made a graceful little speech and his defeated opponent, a pompous little man with a great moustache, made another. Then the mob caught hold of Philip by the legs and arms and carried him in triumph through the streets of Oxford to the Liberal Club from the balcony of which he made another speech, and Lady Ottoline looking very sweet and nice and odd distributed smiles and bows. Then we all went to the Morrells to luncheon. Such are the glories and triumphs of this world. I am glad Philip is an M.P. and equally glad I am not.

The Berensons

Smith was a frequent guest at the Berensons' villa, I Tatti; he helped them choose the original furnishings and he watched it become the great house that it is today. His letters contain many references to it, both while he was visiting there and later when he was recalling it.

TO HIS MOTHER   March 21, 1903

We are all sleepy today as D'Annunzio[1] and the Duse came last night for some music and stayed till 12 o'clock. Mariechen generally has a clock which she winds up when she wants people to go, and as the winding makes a great noise, the hint — if hint isn't too mild a word for it — is always taken. But last night we were in the music room without the clock, so nothing could be done.

[1] Gabriele D'Annunzio (1863–1938), Italian poet, dramatist, novelist, and soldier, and Eleonora Duse (1859–1924), one of the great actresses of her time and equally famous for her liaison with D'Annunzio.

*　*　*

TO HIS SISTER ALYS   April 23, 1906

We are having a most delightful time and Tovey[1] is a most marvelous natural phenomenon. One hardly thinks of him as a person, he is so like the Aurora Borealis darting up into the sky and corruscating in wonderful shapes — a perpetual fountain of shining, illuminating talk, clear as crystal, profound beyond our fathoming and absolutely inexhaustible. One has only to turn the tap and off he goes. B.B. is plainly afraid of him; he spouts occasionally but with a hesitating and timid wave. Kelly and I feel like little puddles, extremely shallow but glad to deepen ourselves as much as we can from the great overflow while Mariechen plunges into the flood and splashes about like a great delighted fish. So, the house sings with music and talk and a Bacchic thrill runs through the corridors.

[1] Sir Donald Francis Tovey (1875–1940), British pianist, composer, and writer on musical subjects.

*　*　*

TO HIS SISTER MARY   May 5, 1906

I enjoyed my visit to I Tatti immensely — it is an enchanted
house, and one where the human ideal of beautiful and cultivated life is more nearly realized than anywhere else I know.

*   *   *

I Tatti

TO HIS SISTER ALYS   January 29, 1920

In spite of strikes and fears of Bolshevism and all the contemporary troubles, life goes on at this villa in great comfort
and leisure — all seems very much as it used to be before the
war, when I stayed here so often — only we are all five years
older, and the trees have grown, the gardens become more
perfect, while we have become less active, less tolerant, less
capable of fresh enthusiasm and illusion.

It's a strange, beautiful, uncanny house, full of great rooms
and corridors and libraries and pictures, and full too of taboos
and distant sound of thunder and imprecation echoing about
the corridors. It is immensely amusing to watch the arrival of
strangers who come intending to make a good impression and
bring upon themselves, without knowing how, the most appalling condemnations. They break the taboos, they go head
over heels into the pitfalls, poor things — sometimes realizing
what they have done, but more often not — and these are the
worst cases!

*   *   *

I Tatti

TO HIS SISTER ALYS   January 9, 1925

It is just like a little court here with favorites and changes of
favors and jealousies — very amusing to look at, and I think
Mariechen and B.B. both enjoy it. [Kenneth] Clark is the
great favorite now and certainly he seems to deserve his favor
— his knowledge and his reading and his power of expressing

himself are certainly prodigious for his age. He likes it here immensely, loves the good talk and appreciates the humor of the situation and his own to the full, and being rich and popular and independent, he is not much concerned as to what happens. I have just left him sitting with the B.B.'s over a portfolio of photographs, emitting opinions about them which they seem to listen to with respect.

*   *   *

I Tatti

TO ROBERT GATHORNE-HARDY   May 8, 1931

I am living happily enough in a corner of this great villa — indoors, most of the time, as it rains almost every day. But there are 40,000 books in the house, and so many of them that I want and ought to read, that I am as it were paralyzed in front of the shelves and don't know where to begin.

I have been coming here every year for many years, and hitherto the house has been full — too full — of tongues and talk, art students, pilgrims, people of fashion, the ticking of typewriters, arguments on aesthetics, and echoes of gossip; but silence has fallen on all that, and the corridors and libraries only echo to my footsteps, as I wander about in the twilight; for all the shutters are closed, the doors barred and locked, and I can't even step into the garden without summonsing a grim porter to let me out. I enjoy the leisure and silence of the long wet days and feel that I could live happily like this forever, but I have to be back in London this month sometime.

*   *   *

I Tatti

TO KENNETH CLARK   1926

You have been greatly missed since your departure from this enchanted castle. I often wish you were here to laugh with me over some of the more amazing incidents . . . All goes on as before; it is Parnassus with some of the aspects of Mount

Sinai, and the thunders of Jehovah often overwhelm the singing of the Muses. The pictures hang where they hung before, and the Giotto has been replaced upon the stairs with no word spoken. Still the library door opens and strange beings make their entrance; but I am getting practiced in the art of fading away, evanescing, being accustomed to much solitude, "the fiery furnace of people," to use a phrase of Henry James', is often too much for me.

Vernon Lee

TO ETHEL SANDS   February 27, 1916

Vernon Lee[1] has come to live in Chelsea — in lodgings in Oakley Street — so Miss Price tells me. She has made herself so unpopular by her war talk that she now, by a great effort, confines herself to strictly neutral subjects. I have heard of her talking for three hours on central heating, on one occasion, and about "boot-trees" on another.

[1] Pen name of Violet Paget (1856–1935), essayist and writer on aesthetics, politics, and Italian art. The reference here is to her extreme pacificism.

The Tom-cats of Bloomsbury

TO CYRIL CONNOLLY   Autumn 1926

I went to Molly's[1] party yesterday — all the young lions, or rather the young tom-cats of Bloomsbury were there, a few older celebrities, trembling for their thrones and reputations among those hoping to replace them, and a few ladies of fashion anxious to be in the intellectual swim. This audience was addressed by a pert, self-confident French boy[2] with a big mouth and a brazen voice who dinned our ears with a galimatias of what I thought pretentious and incomprehensible nonsense, a new gospel of *sur-réalisme* composed of

Freud, Rimbaud, Valéry, Keyserling and Mussolini — an anti-intellectual gospel and attack on reason, chanted and bellowed at us in a kind of figurative and bombastic prose which, though we pretended to follow it, I am sure none of us really understood. The whole thing — the brazen pretentious boy and the anxious pretentious audience, was extremely funny.

[1] Mary MacCarthy, wife of Desmond MacCarthy.
[2] René Crevel (1900–1935), poet who committed suicide.

A London Tea Party

TO HIS SISTER MARY

11 St. Leonard's Terrace
May 15, 1927

London is cold and gloomy, and I much miss the Italian sunshine, and the Italian spring. Your garden must be lovely now. I find it hard to take up English life again — I am not sure that living in Italy isn't perhaps the best solution for the difficult problem of where to spend one's remaining days. The taste of contemporary life produces in one a slight sensation of nausea — all the little sets of utterly unimportant and uninteresting people, and all the second-rate gossip about ephemeral and second-rate literature. But this mood is perhaps the result of going to a tea party at Sybil Colefax's,[1] and seeing all the old flat faces. I met there, among the other exquisite personalities, Harold Acton[2] who has set up in a luxurious flat in London and is becoming quite a figure in the semi-literary semi-fashionable underworld — what a world!

[1] A London hostess noted for the political and literary celebrities at her parties. She was the wife of Sir Arthur Colefax, a lawyer.
[2] Sir Harold Acton (1904–   ), prominent figure in the intellectual life of Oxford in his undergraduate days and in London thereafter. His books include *Memoirs of an Aesthete* (1948) and *Nancy Mitford: A Memoir* (1975).

Little Kindnesses

TO HUGH TREVOR-ROPER

11 St. Leonard's Terrace
November 27, 1944

I haven't seen you or heard of, or from you since your hasty departure from my party for spinsters a few weeks ago. You rushed off without a word to me, as if you didn't like the company. I have that feeling of having got into the wrong set that overcomes one sometimes; but it is just as well not to betray it too clearly. Pardon this hint, but hermits like myself, however holy, retain, deep as may be their retirement from the world, some maxims of worldly wisdom, which, whether prompted by malice or kindness, they are often tempted to convey to the *jeunes féroces* who pay brief visits to their mossy cells. Some such maxims have clamored behind the portcullis of my false teeth when you and other hyenas and jackals have come here on book-plundering expeditions; such platitudes are placed as liberally in my books, at the disposal of anyone who asks for them. The books are free, the price of the platitudes is only 1 penny each. I will now send you a sample — a penny stamp will be accepted in payment.

I noticed (I notice everything) that you talked with Miss Ethel Sands when you met her here; and the next day, when I motored with her to a choice party Lady Colefax gave in her honor, she spoke of you with interest; she had read your book on Archbishop Laud, for she reads everything.

If you liked her (and if you like me, a more profound query) you can do us both one of those little kindnesses which make life more pleasant. This maiden lady is the oldest and nearest of my friends among women; she is the queen of what — after many many, ah, how many disillusions — I have found to be the best company in England. She reigned for years as real Queen (Lady Colefax was only the stage or pantomine Queen) in Chelsea. In her great house near Dorchester, her lovely chateau near Dieppe, I used to spend weeks among the choicest and most interesting of my contemporaries, English, French and American. Her home in Chelsea has been blitzed and her chateau in France has been looted and she is living quietly now in Wiltshire but will return in a few months to Chelsea. In the meantime, I can freely satisfy my book-lending passion by helping her to satisfy her insatiate passion for reading. I used to have three friends to whom I could safely lend books; two remain; and if you wish to rejoin that choice constellation by sending the *Courts and Cabinets* of the good Gooch with a note to Miss Sands, Fyfield House, Marlborough, such an attention would, I know, be welcomed. (But I fear that you have lent this book to one of *your* lady friends.)

Old people are much more pleased and touched than youngsters imagine when the young seem to like them for themselves and not for what they can get out of them, and the young should never be shy of making the first advances. I once asked the most beloved person I know the secret of a social success which drove him away from London to live alone in the country. "If I love people," he said, "I always tell them I love them." Being completely disinterested and with no gleam of an axe to grind about him, he was almost forced, like Max Beerbohm's[1] hero, to cheat at cards to stop the telephone and the doorbell from ringing.

[1] Max Beerbohm (1872–1956), was a caricaturist, essayist, and critic and the author of a satirical novel of Oxford life, *Zuleika Dobson*.

On Asking Favors

TO HUGH TREVOR-ROPER   11 St. Leonard's Terrace
June 16, 1945

I rang up the great Osbert [Sitwell][1] who will be glad to come to luncheon if the memorial service for Lord Desborough that day doesn't interfere. So, I hope we shall see him. I shan't, however, say anything more about his father's book; I asked him about it once, and he said he would try to find a copy for you. I long ago adopted Jeremy Taylor's wise advice — never ask big men for small favors.

[1] His autobiography is discussed on p. 149.

Learning from the Birds

I hope you will enjoy this room and find it propitious for
work. [Clark was arriving at Chilling for a visit.] It makes
a good workshop for phrases; and if you are infected by the
itch for polishing and repolishing them and trying to make
them perfect, I shall take a pleasure in the fact which is not
malicious for I don't know of any other way of life which is
more enjoyable.

You will be perhaps more grateful if you catch another
taste habit which is less attended with danger and also
provides much enjoyment — the habit of watching birds and
listening to their innocent songs. I acquired the habit and
learnt this bird-lore alone, simply with a field glass and a
book, when I was much older than you are. You will need
a glass and will find a row of bird books in the turning-
bookcase in this room. Get to know the wrens and robins and
blackbirds and chaffinches and green finches in the garden
and the goldfinches that nest in the pear tree; and pay attention to that most self-conscious of all artists among birds,
the thrush, which, while I have been polishing my phrases
in bed, has kept on repeating and polishing his, just outside
the bedroom window. He too is engaged in that indefatigable
pursuit of an unattainable perfection which makes the years
pass by so pleasantly.

His Own Writings

The test of a vocation is the love of the drudgery
it involves.

—Afterthoughts

To Logan Pearsall Smith
Who more nobly than you by skilled example has upheld
This stern doctrine of crafty reserve and chastity of style,
Word by word ever testing again and again the polished
  phrase,
Like some Byzantine carver with subtly loving hand
Lingering over his ivory plaque, patiently refining
Curve upon curve, till attained be perfect loveliness and
  strength?
— From *The Collected Works of Robert C. Trevelyan*

Trivia
TO BERTRAND RUSSELL   December 30, 1894

Some day I am going to send you and Alys the scheme of a
little book which I am planning, and get you to help and give
suggestions. I want to illustrate the process of experience —
the way in which gradually one comes to realize the great
facts and laws of life, the incidents which are slight and
humorous, and yet full of significance for thought.

It is very amusing here; dining and talking conventionally
with Sir Edward and Lady Fry — discussing weather and

geography, the Jews in Russia and recent biographies of important people — and then retiring with Roger and one or two of his advanced sisters to talk of very different things. It gives the effect of being in a house where you dine with the towers and battlements and then retire among the sappers, in their secret places, who are undermining it all. The formal figures would be dull, if it were not for the pleasant sense that they are tottering on their bases!

* * *

TO ROBERT C. TREVELYAN

Haslemere
September 28, 1901

I have finished a little book in which I am poaching on the domain of your poets. We prose-writers, I warn you, are going to take over the palaces too long disgraced by the bawdy, high-rouged Muses. They are to be driven out like the Scarlet Woman, with their whoredoms and their cups overflowing with fornications and abominations. With cool, pure streams of prose we shall wash out the places where they have too-long stabled. So your Comus-rout of poets must go. Mine will I hope be the honor of firing the first shot. I hope to enlist Mrs. Sheldon Ames and the Purity League on my side. Who will you have? Jingoes and Licensed Victuallers and the dregs of the music-halls! So at last the old law of Plato shall be enforced, and Poets banished from the perfect state.

* * *

TO HIS SISTER MARY

11 St. Leonard's Terrace
March 26, 1916

Altogether I have given up running this universe, and have expressed my sentiments in the following "Trivia":

I know too much; I have stuffed too many of the facts of history and astronomy into my intellectuals. My eyes have grown dim over books; believing in geological periods and cave dwellers and Chinese dynasties has prematurely aged me.

[121]

Why am I to blame for all that's wrong in the world? I didn't invent Sin and Hate and Slaughter. Who made it my business anyhow to administer the universe and keep the stars to their Copernican courses? My shoulders are bent beneath the weight of the firmament; I grow weary of propping up like Atlas, the vast and erroneous Cosmos.[1]

[1] This, with slight changes, appeared in the 1918 edition of *Trivia*.

* * *

11 St. Leonard's Terrace
TO HIS SISTER MARY   March 13, 1917

I am sending thee a copy of *Trivia*. [This was the first commercial edition.] I haven't any more up here. It is going to be republished with the new ones in the autumn, as Doubleday, Page in America and Constable here have agreed. I get most enthusiastic letters from the American publishers about it.

I am getting on with my selections from Donne's sermons[1] and finding the most magnificent prose scattered here and there in those terrible folios. Most of the sermons are practically unreadable, but now and then he bursts out about death and sin and damnation with a splendour and magnificence that takes one's breath away. I have made friends with Gosse[2] who has been awfully kind in lending me rare first editions. He is a sensitive, polite, [. . . illegible] old bird and most amusing company.

[1] Published as *An Essay on Donne's Sermons* (1919).
[2] Sir Edmund Gosse (1849–1928), critic and man of letters, was one of the best-known writers on the literary scene in London for decades. He wrote biographies of John Donne, Jeremy Taylor, Thomas Gray, Congreve, and Swinburne. He was a close friend of Henry James.

* * *

11 St. Leonard's Terrace
TO HELEN THOMAS FLEXNER   December 27, 1918

I ought to have answered long ago the friendly and beautiful letter, which flew like a bluebird across the Atlantic to my room at the top of our Chelsea house, and sang, and kept on singing in my ears, the pleasantest praise and the most charming memories. Does thee know that when I think of my writing, I often see a picture of thee as I saw thee one summer day, years ago, at Green Hill? I was walking up from High Buildings and I saw thee sitting under a tree in a white spotted dress absorbed in reading; and the thought came to me, "Ah, what a charming thing it would be to write a book that would be thus read under a green tree on a summer day by the charming and fastidious eyes of a lady in a white spotted dress." Thy letter, saying the beautiful things that have given me more pleasure than any other praise, makes me feel that ambition has been crowned with success, and my long un-believed dream has come true; for the tree and the dress are not essential to it, but the fastidious eyes have been pleased by a book of my writing — so all is not vanity and disillusion in this disconcerting existence of ours.

Trivia has had a success over here which has been very pleasant, after the indifference it met with on its first adventure. The three or four people who then liked it, have grown into the thousands, and if my head were younger, it might get a little turned. The encouragement has anyhow helped me to go on with the little experiment and I have written a good deal in the last year or two which will in due time appear in another volume.

*   *   *

11 St. Leonard's Terrace
TO HIS SISTER MARY   June 7, 1922

Thanks for what thee says about *More Trivia* — do tell me sometimes which are the ones thee likes, I always like to hear that. *The Times* review was queer — Desmond MacCarthy has a charming article in the last *New Statesman*.

Santayana writes that he liked *More Trivia* more than *Trivia* as it has all the freshness of the first collection with more wit and more depth. "The whole makes a picture of the self-consciousness of the modern man, which is not only delight-fully vivid and humorous, but is a great *document*; because although it represents only one side of yourself, or of any of us, it is just the side which the age has made conspicuous.

[123]

Men have always been victims of trifles; but when they were uncomfortable and passionate and in constant danger, they hardly had time to notice what the texture of their thoughts was in the calm intervals; whereas with us the intervals are all; and that is what you have painted."

I think that extremely well put.

* * *

11 St. Leonard's Terrace

TO HUGH TREVOR-ROPER   August 19, 1941

I had, as you noticed with devilish penetration, been just slightly chagrined by the parsimony of your pencil marks when looking over *Trivia;* but you have now made most generous amends. *Trivia* is a goddess who loves to be mirrored in the eyes of mortals and her desire is to smile *nei plenilunii sereni* amid the *ninfe eterne.* To find the special grace of her delight silvered in the eyes of a young and contemptuous generation is to feed on the honey of fame, and drink the milk of Paradise in a way that makes her old author feel giddy. My poor little book, scorned and only noticed to be spat upon for so many years by Bloomsbury and Cambridge, and indeed by all my acquaintances, now to find a recognition for the special grace of its delight, and a recognition that seems as if it might endure — this to my mind is to taste of something sweeter than wealth and power — or than revenge, which according to great authorities, is the most delicious morsel at the feast of life. Yes, the flattery you give me is more delicious than any revenge that I can imagine. What return can I make for your bounty? To say that you are a person of exquisite taste would be superogatory since your letter is almost blinding proof of this; but I may add that it is accompanied by gifts of irony and intelligence which make your company the best company in the world. . . .

P.S. To return to *Trivia:* It seems to be written for various tastes. Rose Macaulay selected for her charming anthology the following: High Life, In the Pulpit, The Age, Mammon, Social Success, Above the Clouds, Interruption, The Garden Party, and Shadowed. I think this a good selection and it includes the grandest phrase I ever wrote:

"And with what a holy vehemence would I exclaim and cry out against all forms of doctrinal error — all the execrable hypotheses of the great Heresiarchs!"

*   *   *

11 St. Leonard's Terrace
TO ROBERT GATHORNE-HARDY   August 29, 1941

Gilbert Murray's misprint was "Aegospotamoi" for "Kynoskephalae," in a book published by the Oxford Press, which went through three editions before it was noticed. I wonder if he ever forgave the person who pointed it out; I always bear a grudge against a person who points out a misprint in one of my books, though I try to be grateful, as I know I ought to be. But such things make a writer's path a stony one. However, I get two pounds of butter every week from an Irish admirer, which smooths and softens and oils my path.

As to short stories, I can recommend no model. I used to swear by Guy de Maupassant but can't read him now. Katherine Mansfield is a wash-out, and Chekhov has no art. I found for myself a model in extreme brevity — in "Silvia Doria" in *Trivia* and in "The Vicar of Lynch" and "Sir Eustace Carr" [in *More Trivia*]. But Henry James' "dreadful little question, 'How to do it'," everyone must solve for himself.

*   *   *

11 St. Leonard's Terrace
TO HUGH TREVOR-ROPER   March 14, 1943

Your arch enemy and rival hyena has just spent the night at this hotel and, on my insistence brought back four volumes of a diary I kept during my Arcadizing, when *Trivia* was written and when, a true disciple of Aristippus of Cyrene, of Pater, and of Proust, I noted down in aureate words the golden moments of my rustic, solitary days. How you would growl and spit if you tried to read that record, and with how rude a gesture you would fling the book away, to begin to boast of your participation in those bloodsports which make bearable the English countryside to you.

[125]

But you shall not read this record; you couldn't read it, in fact, I can hardly read it myself — so precious it is, so pretentious, so priggish. And yet, after all, so pretty! But it is not for your eyes. Some of the thoughts noted down in it I will quote for you — I was an early lover of the aphoristic art:

Riches are like sea-water, the more you drink the thirstier you become.

The longer a man's fame is likely to last, the longer will it be in coming.

Great minds are like eagles and build their nests in some lofty solitude.

People with loud voices are almost incapable of subtle thoughts.

Every true artist must live alone and in despair.

Of all people the Greeks have dreamt the dreams of life most wisely.

You will think from these wisecracks that I was clever as well as good. But enough virtue survives in me to make me confess that they are all stolen from Teutonic writers such as foxhunters would never read.

The Eton and Christ Church swan who swam down from Reading, where he is stationed, with these diaries taken when our house was bombed, finding me drifting rudderless on the flood of London life, kindly gave me a few of the rules and maxims which in vain I have begged from others to help me to steer my course, e.g.:

Never be surprised at being surprised at life.

Beware of the hand that feeds you — it will slap you in the face.

If you walk through the grass too often you are bound to leave a path.

* * *

I hope your period of leave is proving pleasant to you and that
your days are thoughtful as well as fishful days. I am rather
under the impression that you are taking a pause or holiday to
consider your future and your fate, to decide what you want
to make of your life, what are your real wishes, and how you
can best attain them. I don't know your exact age but I think
you will soon be out of your twenties, if you haven't already
left that crude, yeasty distressful decade behind you. I take it
that you are about thirty, a turning point in life when one has
more or less to decide on the future path one wants to pursue.
Here we are in life, something has got to be done about it; one
has ventured on various paths which seemed to lead to nothing, snatched at fruit which has turned sour, knocking at doors
that have either remained closed, or, if they have opened, have
led into what seemed likely to be prisons or penitentiaries, or
bordels, from which one must flee to save one's life.

But enough of Methusalesque reflections, though the fact
that I am somewhat older than you are — a half century or
so — will make you pardon my prolixity, I hope. More to the
point will be an account of my experience when I was at the
age which you have now attained. I had gone abroad, after
leaving Oxford, with the intention of following in the footsteps of my fellow expatriate Henry James, had lived four
or five years, as he had lived, in Paris, under the influence of
Flaubert and Guy de Maupassant, spending my days in a
laborious attempt to imitate those masters. In 1896, at the age
of 31, I published a laborious, precious, imitative volume of
short stories of no real merit. The book [*The Youth of Parnassus*] was deservedly a failure — a failure in my own eyes as
well as in those of the few people who tried to read it. I felt
that I had taken the wrong path; but I had found pleasure in
my barren labors and had tasted of what I consider the richest
cake which is baked in the oven of the gods — the ecstasy and
exasperation of the art of writing. To indulge in this sacred
vice in peace, I went to live in the country and spent the
years I describe in my journals writing *Trivia,* which you

pleased me greatly by saying the other day you had re-read with interest. After all, *Trivia* is the center and secret of my life; what else I have done isn't of much importance, but to write this little book was, I think, worth while. No one thought so at the time and the book found practically no readers for many years. This was discouraging, of course, but as I had no inflated notion of my own gifts or pretensions I wasn't made unhappy by this apparent failure of everything I wrote. Now I am pleased that people read and like it. Speaking of *Trivia*, I find that it was believed in antiquity by some authorities that the worship of that goddess was introduced into Italy and established at Aricia by Orestes — you will remember that Martial mentions *Triviae nemorosa regna,* at the eighth milestone from Rome. Other authorities believe that Hippolytus was restored to life by Trivia or Diana and placed by her in the grove of Aricia where Virgil (who holds this view) says that worshippers must only come on foot, since

> templo Triviae lucisque sacratis
> Cornipededes arcentur equi

owing to the misadventure of the son of Theseus. You are more expert in these learned matters than I am, but I like to think that Horace was wrong when he said that Diana was not able to liberate the chaste Hippolytus from the infernal regions. As I feel myself again on the threshold of these regions just at present, I like to believe that the rescue is not impossible. In the meanwhile, if I do go under, I shall take Horace's *Diffugere nives* with me for my melancholy recitation, as I agree with A. E. Housman that it is the finest poem that antiquity has bequeathed us. Ah, to have written those lines would be the highest reward that could adorn a human existence, and the query as to what to do about our brief and transient sojourn on this planet, would require no other answer.

* * *

Edward Weeks (1898–   ), famous as the editor of The Atlantic Monthly *from 1938 to 1966. He wrote his own reminiscenses,* Writers and Friends, *in 1981.*

[128]

TO EDWARD WEEKS

I am really horrified by the time that has elapsed since I received your letter of April 2, and that I never answered it or acknowledged the cheque you so kindly sent me. Owing to paying both American and British tax I am forced to think of money, as the wolf howls at my door now and then, though as yet but faintly. I never used to think at all of such matters . . .

But poverty to pay for paper and stamps is not my excuse for not writing — simply illness and old age. I celebrated my eighty-first birthday last month [he was actually 80 in 1945], and for months before that I was seriously ill. We have had a trying time, and my house was bombed three times. But I am better now, though still bed-ridden.

> "There is much to be said
> For staying in bed"

is my song in this wintry weather.

As I have had no accounts from Little, Brown for the last two or three years, I suppose that the sale of my *Unforgotten Years* has ceased, and that that book and the book on Milton are out of print.

Messrs. Harcourt Brace[1] have been more fortunate with my *Trivia*, which they published in 1918, and which they have now reprinted. This book seems to be enjoying a second blossoming. I planted the little tree with the fantastic notion that it might live on and flower after my decease, and there are pleasant moments when I feel I haven't utterly failed in this ambition. That *All Trivia* has been reprinted ten or twelve times in the last twenty-eight years, and that passages from it were read in the House of Lords a few weeks ago, and that Harcourt Brace's new issue seems to be booming in America (I have just received a laudation of it by Christopher Morley in the Book-of-the-Month Review for December, and one in *Time* for December 10th) encourage this flattering notion.

"Author Smith," as he is called in *Time*, hopes that Editor Weeks will give a glance at this new issue, which contains many subtle changes. I have brooded for years and mooned over the little book, giving it "those final gossamer touches and tendernesses" which that exquisite painter and contemporary of Blake's, Samuel Palmer, whose pictures are priceless now, compared to the "few last sun glows which give the fruits of their sweetness." Until these touches and tendernesses had been given, he refused to sell his pictures, though he lived in extreme poverty. So I refused for years to publish *Trivia*; and when it was at last published in 1902, it had to wait sixteen years before it found more than three or four readers.

To return, after this burst of octogenarian boasting, to the queries in your letter.

You ask me what I thought of Santayana's two volumes of autobiography. [*The Background of My Life* (1944) and *The Middle Span* (1945) were the first two volumes of Santayana's autobiography, *Persons and Places*.] Frankly, I was disappointed and thought them rather sour and ungenerous in tone. One should take leave of life with a more genial grace. I think he will live as an essayist and above all a letter writer. I printed one of his letters in my *Unforgotten Years* and in rummaging through my old papers I have found a good many more, which he has given me permission to print. I found also a number of letters from Henry James and from Robert Bridges, and a beautiful unpublished epistle in verse by Bridges *On Receiving Trivia from the Author*.[2] These too I have permission to print and have thought of making a book of them one day.

I found also my correspondence with Virginia Woolf. This is being soon printed in a miscellany called *Orion,* and I will send you a copy if I can get one. But I don't think you will want to print it, as the fear of our fierce laws of libel has forced me to leave out a good deal of the spice which makes the correspondence between two not unmalicious persons as Virginia and myself of interest. But of course you can print it if you want to.

What oddly enough I do find is that best of all these letters are those of Hannah Whitall Smith, my own mother. It appears (what I didn't know) that H.W.S. was the authoress of what is established now as a little religious classic, *The*

Christian's Secret of a Happy Life, which, written seventy years ago, was translated into every language of Europe and into Chinese and Japanese. This book made her world famous at the time, and that fame has lasted since after selling more than a million copies in the United States alone, her American publishers still sell five or six thousand copies every year. Her English publisher, Bertram Christian, has read these familiar letters with great pleasure and has asked me to edit for his firm [Nisbet] a selection from them and on this task I am now engaged. This rich and witty old Quaker lady happened to possess a fine-pointed pen of gold, and her letters are extremely amusing as well as full of ripe wisdom and tenderness and charm. My mother, the mother of Mrs. Bertrand Russell and of the wife of the famous art critic, Berenson, and of myself, came in contact with many Europeans and Americans of interest.

I printed extracts from two of her letters in my *Unforgotten Years* and she is the real heroine and most living character in that book.

H.W.S. was born over a hundred years ago (1832). Her first letter was written from the very heart of Philadelphia Quakerism in 1847; her last sixty-four years later (1911) from the country house on the Thames, near Oxford.

[1] Actually, *Trivia* was published by Doubleday, Page and Company in 1918. Harcourt, Brace and Company brought out *More Trivia* in 1921, *Afterthoughts* in 1931, and *All Trivia,* including "Last Words," in 1934 and, in a new edition, in 1945.

[2] This was the poem, privately printed in 1930 by Robert Gathorne-Hardy at The Mill House Press, Stanford Dingley, in thirty-six copies:

On Receiving Trivia from the Author
by Robert Bridges

The Manor House,
Yattendon, Berkshire, 1903

When I imagine your select society
    Abounding in clever fellows
Alert to warn you, Logan, — airing their morals
    In frankly spoken friendliness, —
That you as indolently as any grasshopper,
    Are wasting all your fair summer,

'Tis idle in me fancying you may resent
  My kindly judgement, nor can I
Pretend an empty scruple in dispensing it:
  For flattery, that poisons a fool,
Should yet from folly quickly discourage the wise.
  And surely you have full leisure
And wisdom ample for reflection of spirit,
  Whether in retirement of Surrey
You sip the scented honey of English country-life,
  Anon, departed with the birds,
Beneath Italian skies pleasantly wintering,
  Call Firenze your mother,
Or are met idly loitering in Oxford again
  'Mong colleges and old libraries.
I set out not to praise a worldly ambition,
  Though needful as riches to man,
Nay though to finest gold it is transmutable,
  To silver or paper money;

It is commonly seen amongst us; I desire
  That it ever increase and flourish,
That each, his own idea serving endeavour
  To win the happiness of having,
Whether it be merely riches or public renown,
  Place of minister or bishop,
Throne in the city or in the university,
  — Lord Mayor or Vice Chancellor, —
To lead an army, or with orchestral baton
  Command a campaign of fiddles;
Let each attain his fancy: see him at the end
  Involved in incessant affairs
Far more annoying than the forgotten trouble
  Expended in gaining the prize:
Is not one only feeling in the heart of all?
  Then do not all speak poetry?
And fall to praising country life, the ecstasies
  Of Earth's abundant arch-delight,
Of lonely contemplation, of hallowed leisure,
  The music and peace of the soul?

If this be every ambition's last ambition,
  The word of all experience,
Small blame to him who early findest & loveth
  What all return to in the end.

*　*　*

11 St. Leonard's Terrace
December 23, 1945

I am sending you my most dismal good wishes for this dreariest of all seasons, and also my own news, which is of interest to me at least. Since neither my doctor nor you will give me a death certificate, I have been packed back from the realms of Persephone — permits-of-stay there are now limited in date. My doctor I can understand as I am a regular source of income to him although why you should desire (or seem to desire) my return from the realms of Tartarus and gloomy Dis is a mystery, though a pleasant mystery, to me, and the pleasure I take in your conversation is a large ingredient in my desire to return. To reward you I have two Christmas presents for you, one to be presented in a friendly spirit, the other in malice prepense, if you know what that is.

The friendly gift is the new revised, revived, re-adorned redecorated re-alembicated edition of *Trivia*. . . .

If you ever have occasion to write an obituary notice of me, you can say that realizing in my youth that I had little or no literary talent, I was taken by the fantastic notion that I might write one little book that might live on beyond my decease. I flatter myself just now that I haven't failed altogether — the new edition has blossomed again all over America; and across the irremeable oceans the trumpet blasts of my triumph sound faintly (and not unpleasantly) in my ears. And in England too I hear that the pages of *All Trivia* were read (I think by Lord Cranborne) in the House of Lords, but I haven't bothered to look up the reference in *The Times*. Can you outboast this? . . .

The other gift I hope to give you is malicious in intent, six volumes of what I hold to be the best history in English after Gibbon. I have read it five or six times; you I know haven't read it once, and you won't read it now, since Oxford history tutors (I have known many of them) are too busy tutoring dullards and trying to turn sows' ears into silk purses to read. Often have I listened to Freeman,[1] Vinogradoff,[2] and Firth[3] discourse on this and even the official defender of the tutors,

Herbert Fisher,[4] wouldn't and couldn't deny the indictment.

[1] Edward Augustus Freeman (1823–1892), historian and Oxford professor.
[2] Sir Paul Vinogradoff (1854–1925), a native of Russia who taught at Oxford for many years and was one of the world's great authorities on the English common law.
[3] Sir Charles Harding Firth (1857–1936), historian and Oxford professor.
[4] H.A.L. Fisher (1865–1940), historian and statesman chiefly remembered for his *History of Europe,* three volumes (1935). After serving as British delegate to the League of Nations he returned to Oxford where he was warden of New College until his death.

The Life and Letters of Sir Henry Wotton

44 Grosvenor Road, London
TO HELEN THOMAS FLEXNER   July 13, 1901

I have somehow engaged myself in a piece of solid "work" of a half-historical kind — I am collecting and reprinting Sir Henry Wotton's letters and have been hunting among Government Records and Bodleian manuscripts and old college libraries. I love the man and the period — he started out under Elizabeth, was James' ambassador at Venice, and then spent the last years of a beautiful old age as Provost of Eton — a courtier, scholar, poet, wit and at last a kindly old saint — it is a real pleasure to find among old dust-heaps some trace of him; and when I untie a great bundle of manuscripts and at last come upon his beautiful clear handwriting and some account of his feelings and adventures — so alive, so humorous and charming among dead intrigues and diplomacies, it is as delightful and exciting as the sight of a friend in the crowd of a foreign city. And there is pleasure too in dry dates and details, in going straight to the documents and finding out how glaring the mistakes are of all your predecessors. I feel that [much] of the pleasure of middle life is literary-historical squabbling — venomous, self-righteous attacks on people like Gosse and Sidney Lee[1] — letters in the Athenaeum full of dates and corrections. Love of money, love of fame, love of work, love of pedantry — these, with love of the world, are among the dangerous bypaths in which one can wander fatally and far — which one tempts thee most? I am always wondering about life, and what we are all here for on this Star. But I wonder more about aesthetic problems, I think.

[1] Sir Sidney Lee (1859–1926), principal editor of *The Dictionary of National Biography,* author of many critical and scholarly books, and the official biographer of King Edward VII.

* * *

Friday's Hill, Haslemere
TO HELEN THOMAS FLEXNER October 18, 1902

I am plodding away at my old Ambassador, and begin to realize how insidious is the great temptation of middle age — I mean work, dry, regular-work, which kills the spirit, but fills the mind with self-satisfaction. Perhaps though, one ought to be grateful that there is the refuge of pedantry for the poor middle years, today is my birthday [he was 37] and I feel the burden of time heavy on my back. However, I plan some personal, half . . . [illegible] essays to make a little book when my two volumes [on Henry Wotton] are finished. I think it will be fun.

My reading is all in the Seventeenth century now — Shakespeare, Bacon, Jeremy Taylor and various historians. I love the time, the rich language, the magnanimity of the people, the aristocratic state of life, the palaces and formal gardens of the Italianized England, with Van Dyck's people to inhabit them, and all in the mellow glow of the long afternoon of the English Renaissance.

* * *

2 Bath Place, Oxford
TO HIS SISTER ALYS December 5, 1902

I am hunting up all sorts of obscure points for my book, and my mind is becoming a kind of Elizabethan junkshop. I am amazed that I can not only do it but take an interest, a vivid interest in it all. I would give a good deal to find out who a person named Higgins was who lived in Venice about 1604 —

fancy in a world with so many important things in it, bothering one's head about a remote dead and no doubt utterly unimportant Higgins!

* * *

I have a space for moral reflections:
   I am revelling in pedantry. There is pleasure in it like I imagine the pleasure of needlework — it fills the time, gives me a sense of work, and does not tax the brain.

* * *

I really am enjoying my work in the old library, though it is of the dullest description. I consult with funny old bookworms and enjoy my insight and welcome into the world of Dryasdust scholars.

* * *

I am trying to get my book into shape and find it most difficult to write plain expository prose. Having never practiced writing the obvious, I long for gifts of journalists, who can write a plain, common sense statement of facts and reflections. Can Bertie be obvious when he treats of the fiscal question or does he make it subtle and complicated?

M. Carey Thomas (1858–1935) was a first cousin of Smith's, a daughter of Hannah Smith's sister Mary Thomas of Baltimore, and a sister of Helen Thomas Flexner. She had an early influence on Smith, urging him to give up business and to live and study abroad. He was always grateful to her for the advice and wrote to her often about his intellectual interests. She was for many years president of Bryn Mawr College.

Iffley, Oxford
April 25, 1908

Thank thee very much for thy kind letter about my book. No one is more surprised than I at its reception, and no one of course is more pleased — unless indeed I except Auntie Lill[1] who, in the false perspective of Germantown, seems to think that a star of glory has descended on the Smith family!

But thy approval is harder to win, and much more valuable and pleasant in proportion. The book indeed should have been dedicated to thee, for probably without thee it would never have been written. Thee it was who exploded the bomb that shattered my prison walls. I hear the reverberations of it still and wonder at and greatly admire thy courage. I am glad to think that I have not given thee cause to regret it, and I hope thee keeps the bomb ready to explode on other suitable occasions. It was thee who first opened for me the door out, who set the standard, who lit the torch, and but for thee I tremble to think what the rest of us would have become. I wish I knew more precisely how *thee* started, and whether anyone exploded a bomb for thee?

To return to Sir Henry Wotton — I was indeed lucky, as thee says, to find such a charming subject for biography — one could not have wished for a more sympathetic companion, or a more beautiful world. I had long been interested in him, but had no idea, that about so familiar a figure, there were such masses of unknown information to be found. I could write a pleasing little essay, if such things were worthwhile, on the methods of English historians. As far as I know there is only James Spedding's *Life* of Bacon in the Elizabethan period which has been honestly done.

Thee certainly has imposed on thyself a tremendous penance in reading all of Mrs. Humphrey Ward, and to be frank, I can't help thinking that it is one that fits the crime! Did I really talk against Henry James? If I did I must retract it now — he is a figure that grows in the imagination with each new book, and I think that in the last ten years he has jumped into undoubted greatness. I love to lose myself in darkest James and ever discover new marvels there.

I wonder if I can tell thee of any books thee does not know? I have just read a book, an American book of the Hawthorne period which I put very high, Herman Melville's *Moby Dick*. I wonder if thee knows it? Conrad's *Lord Jim* I consider a work of genius, and Edmund Gosse's *Father and Son* is fascinating reading. I have just read a very clever novel not up to James or Conrad, but much above the ordinary run, *Valerie Upton* by Miss [Anne Douglas] Sedgwick — published I believe in America under the title *A Fountain Unsealed [A Fountain Sealed]*. I am now deep in Anatole France's *Jeanne d'Arc*, which is delightful, and I have on hand Maxime du Camp's *Souvenirs Littéraires*, interesting for his accounts of Flaubert and George Sand. Other books I have read more or less recently and can recommend are Henry Sedgwick's *Life*, Lady Burne-Jones' charming life of her husband[2]; Fielding-Hall's *Soul of a People*[3] (a classic by the way) and March Phillipps' *Desert*.[4] [W. H.] Hudson's *Naturalist in La Plata* is another classic, and there is an esoteric cult for his novel *Green Mansions*, about which I am afraid I am a heretic, but his *Purple Land* I liked very much. I have also on hand Karl Justi's great work on *Winckelmann und seine Zeitgenossen*.[5] Berenson was full of it when I saw him in Italy last month.

[1] Robert Pearsall Smith's unmarried sister Elizabeth (1825–1913) was called Auntie Lill by members of her family. She lived in Philadelphia and was the center of the family's efforts to keep their association with that city. She became in their eyes amiably provincial.

[2] *Memorials of Edward Burne-Jones* was written by Georgiana, the wife of the famous painter and designer.

[3] *The Soul of a People* by Harold Fielding-Hall was a study of the life and beliefs of the Burmese.

[4] *In the Desert: The Hinterland of Algiers* was published in 1905 and the author was Lisle March Phillipps (1863–1917).

[5] This three-volume biography of J. J. Winckelmann, the great German founder of modern studies of Greek sculpture and antiquities, was by Karl Justi (1832–1912). It was published in 1898.

The Golden Grove: Selections from Jeremy Taylor

TO ROBERT GATHORNE-HARDY   April 1929

When I read the proofs I hated the article [on Jeremy Taylor
in the magazine *Life and Letters*] and thought it wretched
and worthless; but it may be better than I think. There is no
blacker moment than when one first sees a piece of one's own
prose in print. Later on it may shimmer and gleam again, but
the first sight of it is awful.

There is another awful meditation that visits me sometimes when I lie awake at night — the fearful thought namely
that when *The Golden Grove* is published, you will point
out to me lovely passages that I have overlooked and omitted.
That nightingale you quoted sings in my ears a dolorous
song — I haven't dared look up the passage.[1]

[1] This was the sentence Smith had not included in his selections from
Taylor:

> "To be filling the roomes of the understanding and aery and in-
> effective notions is just such an excellency, as it is in a man to
> imitate the voice of birds; at his very best the Nightingale shall
> excel him."

*   *   *

TO ROBERT GATHORNE-HARDY   April 11, 1929

. . . ominous to my mind is the fact that the BBC is taking up
the subject [of sermons as literature] and will begin next
month to bellow through space fine passages from old sermons.
They offered me some nice money — which I am glad to say
I refused — to write in the *Radio Times* a popular introduction to the series. I am by nature a lover of unfrequented
shrines, and when the crowds arrive with their litter I am
tempted to turn to other altars. Am I to blame for leading on
the crowd? My author's vanity — and his vanity is the canker
and curse of an author's life — flatters me by saying that I
am to blame, but my common sense answers this with the
melancholy reflection that we are all Time's children and
simply discover what is already in the air. We keep at the most
but a few days ahead of the crowd, which would arrive anyhow without our leading. So if a Jeremy Taylor boom is upon

us, you and I cannot be blamed and can console ourselves with the rise in value of our volumes.

I am returning to London and will come to see you at Conduit Street. I want to have a serious talk with you about a certain old Bishop of Norwich [Joseph Hall] whose works in an immense folio of 1,400 pages I bought the other day in Southampton, and am now busy in reading.

"God and his Angels sit upon the scaffolds of Heaven and regard us —— "

"If there be any sons of Thunder amongst you; if you ever rattled the terrible judgment of God upon sinners —— "

"I am a stranger even at home; therefore if the dogs of the world bark at me, I neither care nor wonder —— "

that's how he writes but I dare say you know all about him — though I am sure the BBC doesn't.

* * *

In May 1929 Edmund Gosse's library was sold at Sotheby's and in the auction were some books by Jeremy Taylor, including The Golden Grove, *a manual of daily prayers.*

TO ROBERT GATHORNE-HARDY   May 3, 1929

I feel this of the Jeremy Taylors. I must have *The Golden Grove;* I once had it in my possession for some time and would now like to possess it until I join the former owner on the further side of the grave. As I think I have told you, I miss Gosse much more than I expected to, for I didn't know him intimately, wasn't very fond of him, and wouldn't have trusted him around the corner. But we had tastes in common, and that, for people with tastes, is one of the strongest of bonds. I find that among those who have played that vanishing trick called dying on me, it is to the ones who shared my thoughts that my thoughts keep most constantly turning; and Gosse has taken his place in this company. So if you bid on my behalf for *The Golden Grove* (as you kindly said you would) don't let any reasonable price deter you.

* * *

The Golden Grove *was sold to Smith and he expressed his pleasure:*

I took great delight in the long-desired book; it slept beside me (not with me); I woke up to read the description on p. 42 of the joys of Heaven — joys which I shall taste before you do, as I am so much nearer that golden threshold.

And yet how difficult it is to possess one's possessions! Mine elude me and still keep aloof. I cannot really appropriate them and make them mine, save in the rarest and briefest moments. Perhaps your method of going to bed with them is the best.

I think you said you were reading [Bishop Joseph] Hall — do look out for aphorisms and pithy sentences with which he enriches his pages. Those that I have collected from him make me want to find some more. Also out-of-the-way iniquities — the two I discovered "polluting the house of God with abominable altars" and "singing with Nero while the city burns" have been a great delight to my criminal imagination, though neither of them quite equals the giant sin that so took Donne's giant fancy.

My soul is at present feeding on a strangely beautiful and purple patch I found in *The Times* last Thursday, where its Manila correspondent, after an arid description of the sun's eclipse, suddenly cabled: "The weather was cloudless, the conditions were perfect. Acacia trees closed their leaves as for the night; dew fell, chickens roosted, and the peasants in the outlying villages, terrified by the awful phenomenon, supplicated the saints."

Could this sentence, which Flaubert might have written with the help of Gibbon, be the chance product of a journalist's pen? I cannot think so.

Unforgotten Years

Unforgotten Years was the most successful of Smith's books published in America. Chapters from it appeared in The Atlantic Monthly *from July 1937 to August 1938, and it became the January 1939 selection of the Book-of-the-Month Club, which gave it a huge sale. It was widely — and favorably — reviewed, bringing the author to the attention of a public that had not been aware of his earlier books of literary essays. It was published in England by Constable and Co., in 1938 and was widely noticed there too.*

TO ROBERT GATHORNE-HARDY   October 12, 1938

I have just received the American edition of my *Unforgotten Years*. They have got it up beautifully, and say that it has been chosen as the Book-of-the-Month in America, which means, before they begin to boom(?) it, a sale of 100,000 copies. To have written a best seller is a cloud on my declining years, but a cloud which has a silver, or rather a golden, lining which will help me to bear the disgrace.

*   *   *

                                    11 St. Leonard's Terrace
TO HUGH TREVOR-ROPER   January 14, 1943

This very afternoon, sent by that Prince Charming of the War Office, James Pope-Hennessy, a Triviolator "just down from the staff college" (whatever that means) is coming to throw himself upon the bosom (metaphorically speaking) of the writer of a book you may have heard of, and of an autobiography which the youth told the above-mentioned Prince Charming was one of the two best modern autobiographies. Why two? "Why drag in Velasquez?" as Whistler said. I was once told by Raymond Mortimer, or someone who often went to Paris, that he had heard André Gide say that there were only two English writers in whom he took any interest. One was me. Like a bloody fool, I asked who was the other, hoping he would mention Max Beerbohm or Robert Bridges, but the reply, "Middleton Murry"[1] has darkened my life ever

since. Now if I ask my visitor today who is the second autobiographer and he says "Beverley Nichols"[2] or "Marie Stopes"[3]
(as it is quite possible that he will) you will inherit my dictionaries next week.[4]

My most exquisite taste I have just been gratifying by reading the *Princesse de Babylone* by Voltaire,[5] of which I dare
say you have never heard. It's the most enchanting story I have
ever read. It suggests to me the problem now before me which
is how to spend the tag end of the life which my doctor
promises me, namely two and a half years. Shall I spend it
reading Voltaire, or reading Goethe, or writing illegible letters
to you? You once promised to guide my aged footsteps to a
dignified and worthy end. Now is a chance to give me good
advice. I will do whatever you think best.

[1] John Middleton Murry (1889–1957), prolific British literary critic
and husband of Katherine Mansfield.
[2] Beverley Nichols (1900–1983), author of more than sixty books,
from novels and plays to books of essays on gardening and life in the
country, and a serious book on India, mentioned later.
[3] Marie Stopes wrote popular sex manuals, the most famous being
Married Love, which sold millions of copies.
[4] Smith had told Trevor-Roper that he was going to leave him his
dictionaries, a promise he kept.
[5] A burlesque romance written by Voltaire when he was seventy-four
years old.

Unforgotten Years: AN EXCHANGE

TO LOGAN PEARSALL SMITH   December 20, 1938

I have just been reading *Unforgotten Years* with great pleasure, but have made a serious discovery about you. My study
of Greek Drama enables me to detect the workings of a
hereditary δαίμων or ἀλάστωρ [demon or spirit], and I see to
my horror that you have only escaped from the religious and
moral idealism of your ancestors, to fall into the same idealism
or idolatry under a slight disguise. You pursue style and
beauty of language with the same blind devotion as your
parents pursued salvation.

[143]

You will have to begin your life over again, and write those great books in a more chastened spirit. I find that my great books also are waiting to be written.

Gilbert Murray

11 St. Leonard's Terrace

TO GILBERT MURRAY   January 1, 1939

Thank you for your note. I think you are right; I am cursed by the hereditary danger of preaching, only, unlike my parents, nobody listens to my exhortations.

I hope that among the great books you are still to write that there will be a volume at least of reminiscences.

Logan Pearsall Smith

Milton and His Modern Critics

11 St. Leonard's Terrace

TO EDWARD WEEKS   April 8, 1940

I have just written an essay called *Milton Dethroned*[1] describing how two penniless young Americans from the Middle and further West arrived in London about 1908, knowing no one, and without introductions, but determined to conquer London; how they more or less achieved their purpose, largely by attempting to dim the luster of the star of Milton and dislodge him from his throne in Heaven. Their names were Ezra Pound and T. S. Eliot. Where Pound was born I can't find out, but Eliot came from St. Louis, so he writes me, but his grandfather was a Bostonian. The late President Eliot of Harvard belonged, he tells me, to a younger branch of the family.

These adventurous youths made their way fairly quickly, for they were astute and clever: the *jeunes féroces* of London found a leader in Eliot while Ezra Pound, dressed as a cowboy, terrified London with his cowboy whip. They proceeded to conquer Cambridge University (in which Milton has always been hated) and in ten years sixteen readers in English there

[144]

wrote that the dislodgement of Milton had been "accomplished with very little fuss." I have written a somewhat ironic history of this American invasion for a little Oxford Society for Pure English, which was founded by Robert Bridges and myself and it will be published before long by the Oxford University Press. As it will be circulated principally among the few hundred members of the society (though the Press will sell a few copies to outsiders) it occurred to me that you might like me to send you a copy of the mss in case you might like to consider it for the *Atlantic*. It is however too long, I am afraid and anyhow I believe it is difficult to send mss across the Atlantic without government permission and I being an invalid cannot bother about getting that.

[1] This was published as a book, *Milton and His Modern Critics,* by the Atlantic Monthly Press–Little, Brown and Company in 1941.

Smith was keenly interested at all times in the appearance of his books, and he expressed his appreciation of the fine bookmaking that went into the Milton book in this letter to Chester Kerr, then director of the Atlantic Monthly Press.

11 St. Leonard's Terrace
TO CHESTER KERR   May 4, 1941

Your note of April 18th has reached me, after a remarkably quick crossing of the now voracious Atlantic; which expanse of water, by the way, must have swallowed two of the three packets of the American edition of my little book on Milton, as only one, containing two copies, reached these embattled shores. Well, I hope the fishes are enjoying the others and do not find my writing too far above their heads.

Of course I shall be delighted if you will give the MS. of the book to Yale — the war cry of my youth, "To hell with Yale!" — has long since been replaced on my lips with much more reticent outcries. What they are at the present crisis you can easily imagine.

I carry on a brisk and somewhat vituperative correspondence with the Oxford University Press — with brother Chapman, brother Humphrey Milford and brother [Kenneth] Sisam (who is the real power behind the throne), accusing them of all sorts of misdemeanors, and threatening to come to Oxford and break their windows, and all three of them retaliate in kind. Luckily I have no windows to break now, owing to what we call politely "enemy action", so I sent them without fear of grave reprisal your beautiful edition of my little book on Milton, in the knowledge that this exquisite piece of book-production would make them ashamed of their own shabby and cheap printing of it. You will see, by the enclosed bit of a letter from Kenneth Sisam, that the blow has gone home; their only reply worth considering being an attack on your printer's system (or non-system) of word division. I enclose herewith a portion of Sisam's criticisms of your printer, which may be of interest to the Atlantic Press, as Sisam is the acknowledged authority over here on this delicate point, and has written an authoritative essay on the subject which our Society for Pure English printed in its Tract XXIII (Clarendon Press, 1929). And this brings me to the subject of misprints, which are to me points producing an agony like that of boils behind which make it painful for me to sit down. I enclose a note herewith on this distressing subject as I have found some new slips in your edition of my book, for most of which though not all I fear the blame is mine. If there is a touch of acrimony in my notes put it down (and forgive it if you can) to my annoyance at being confined by "enemy action" to one of the dark corners of my house.

To speak of pleasanter matters, I have been amused this morning by receiving a review in *Time* (March 17) of my little book, with the slogan, "Why Does Ezra Pound?" I don't as a rule read the reviews of my books, since if they are praised, I find the praise fatuous, while if they attack me I am annoyed. But a clever review, like this one with a sting in it, I enjoy reading, so if any others of this sort come your way, it would be kind of you to forward them to me. But please don't bother about this. My English reviews I haven't read, though I am told they mostly praise the book. The Cambridge critics are furious, I believe, but I wrote on purpose to annoy them. The Clarendon Press is advertising the book quoting a phrase from Naomi Royde-Smith's review in *Time and Tide*:

"His arraignment of Milton's detractors could not be bettered in deadly malice." I have now sent them (to be used if they want to) a clerihew[1] as we call them, by Lady Witt, wife of the art critic Sir Robert Witt:

> [Messrs Eliot and Pound
> Proclaim doctrines unsound
> In their heresy built on
> Dispraise of John Milton.]

[1] A *clerihew* is a short (4-line) verse form invented by Edmund Cleri-hew Bentley, best known as E. C. Bentley, the author of the classic detective story *Trent's Last Case*.

Looking for
New Writers

The reason why so few good books are written
is that so few people who can write know anything.

— Walter Bagehot

The publication of Unforgotten Years *brought Smith two
new friends and correspondents, Edward Weeks and Ellery
Sedgwick, editors of the* Atlantic Monthly *and of the* Atlantic
Monthly Press *of Little, Brown and Company. Smith's
letters to them were mainly about the literary scene in England since the two Boston editors had asked him to watch
for new writers they might like to publish in America.*

A Cornish Carlyle

11 St. Leonard's Terrace

TO ELLERY SEDGWICK   July 17, 1942

I believe you like to hear of any writing which is both new
and good. Of things of this kind I find little or nothing to
write. Virginia Woolf's volume of posthumous essays[1] is
really enchanting, and E. M. Forster's lecture about her is
an excellent piece of writing. People speak highly of Elizabeth Bowen's *Bowen's Court*, but I haven't read it yet. What
seems like a murky, yet genuine star (if of small magnitude)

has been noticed on our horizon — the son of Cornish peasants and now a fellow of All Souls, A. L. Rowse by name, who has won the reputation of a sound historian by his *Tudor Cornwall* and now what is almost fame by the story of his youth — *A Cornish Childhood* — a perverse and not very pleasant book but the book of a genuine writer — a little Cornish Carlyle in fact, who may grow more mellow with the years.

My wild young friend Cyril Connolly has been taken up by the Astors and made literary editor of the *Sunday Observer* which they own.

[1] *The Death of the Moth* published in 1942.

A Richly Spiced Confection

11 St. Leonard's Terrace

TO EDWARD WEEKS   July 12, 1943

I am writing to you now about another enormous, richly spiced and sugared confection on which I have been eagerly feasting, and it has occurred to me that you and your *Atlantic* readers might like a taste of this great cake also. It consists of the fascinating and frank autobiography[1] of one of the most fascinating members of a strange, incredibly aristocratic family, the Sitwells of Renishaw Hall. The head of the family, Sir George Sitwell, a grand gentleman and a great scholar, died last week in Switzerland, and my friend Sir Osbert, has just inherited the title and the family estates. The daughter, Miss Edith Sitwell, is revealing more and more a touch of genius in her high, almost hysterical screams, and her *A Poet's Notebook,* has been one of the successes of the publishing season here. Sacheverell Sitwell is well known as a poet also but it is the eldest brother of these three large, blonde, passionately-lettered aristocrats (descendants of the author of *Beowulf* and of George IV) who is the real genius of the family and it is his autobiography which has just been sent me in proof. I find it full of fascinating reading, admirable portraits of his grandparents, great aunts and uncles, of their great houses and the strange lives they led in them.

[149]

Much also of historical and literary interest, too. The book is finished but there may be a delay in publication here, so if you would like to see the proofs or selections from them, he would be delighted to let you see them.

I think I can honestly recommend this frank (too frank?) beautifully written and excessively amusing book to you. I think the American public would enjoy meeting these clever and almost incredible products of the rich soil of English life and letters.

¹ *Left Hand, Right Hand,* the first volume of the autobiography of Sir Osbert Sitwell (1892–1969), published by the Atlantic Monthly Press–Little, Brown and Company in 1944.

The Unquiet Grave

11 St. Leonard's Terrace

TO EDWARD WEEKS   January 5, 1944

I have received from the *Atlantic* a delightful Christmas packet, which was most welcome, especially under existing circumstances.¹ What our circumstances are, I daresay you know from the American papers. I must thank you for the kind reminder that I am not forgotten. As I wrote you a couple of months ago, I miss very much not having seen the *Atlantic* for the last eight months, and all my friends, to whom I used to pass it on, complain to me bitterly. I can't by law send money to America; Little, Brown, who used to pay my subscription out of the sale of my books, must have ceased to pay it, as the sale of my book has ceased, I suppose. But I do miss the *Atlantic!*

I am sending you under another cover an article by Raymond Mortimer on Cyril Connolly's brilliant book *Palinurus* which is having such a success here.² You will remember meeting these two writers here at tea one day.

On the reverse of Mortimer's review is an article by a young Captain Pope-Hennessy on whom I would advise you to keep an eye.³ He is a born writer, certainly with "ink in his stomach," as the Chinese say. His book *London Fabric* had a great and well-deserved success a year or two ago.

I saw two people yesterday who regard you as their friend and asked warmly for your news. The great Osbert and the great Edith [Sitwell]. Osbert's book isn't out yet in England but casts its shadow before publication, and there was a great gathering at a picture exhibition — Renishaw and the Renishaw country painted by a brilliant young artist, John Piper. All the Sitwells were there.

I am reading with great delight Matthiessen's excellent book on Henry James,[4] a fine piece of critical work on the latest and greatest period of James' works, which you have read no doubt. I wonder if you have read what I think (and Miss Sitwell agrees with me) the most important novel written in English since *The Golden Bowl* — Rosamond Lehmann's *The Ballad and the Source?*

[1] Weeks had sent him a fruitcake.
[2] *The Unquiet Grave,* a collection of pensées, aphorisms, and quotations published under the pen name Palinurus.
[3] This was James Pope-Hennessy, author of books on Trollope, Robert Louis Stevenson, and Monckton Milnes.
[4] *Henry James: The Major Phase* by F. O. Matthiessen (1944).

Some Good Books

11 St. Leonard's Terrace

TO EDWARD WEEKS   December 4, 1944

It may interest you to hear what I and my friends have been reading with most interest:

First, I should put Rosamond Lehmann's *The Ballad and the Source.* I haven't cared much for her *Dusty Answer* and other previous work and I don't know the lady, but this last book has impressed me immensely. I annoy other writers by declaring that it interests me more than any novel published since Henry James' *Golden Bowl.* And I find that people like Rose Macaulay and Sir Edward Marsh admire it greatly.

Next in interest I put Beverley Nichols' *Survey of India* which is raising havoc and a veritable storm of fury and admiration. I don't like the author or his previous publications but when I had once taken up this frank account of what he saw in India I couldn't put it down.

Another book of even more profound interest is *U.S.S.R. The Story of Soviet Russia* by Walter Duranty. He is an American journalist, I believe [*The New York Times*] who tells the truth about Stalin and the Russians.

Then Cyril — the great Cyril Connolly! His *Unquiet Grave* was out last week and is already unprocurable. He has become the wonder and delight of the best company in London, not only the King of the Great World, as our Osbert describes him, but the dictator of taste among the *jeunes féroces* of the new generation. There has been in his *Horizon* [Connolly was then editing that magazine] a good deal of what I consider pretentious nonsense but the last numbers I have thought excellent and I think you might do well to consider for the *Atlantic* Philip Toynbee's admirable survey of contemporary French literature in the last number. Cyril puts his money on young Toynbee (a grandson of Gilbert Murray's) as destined to be famous.

In the number before there is a really important *Letter to a Young Painter* by a friend of mine Gathorne-Hardy[1] who is that rare phenomenon, an aristocrat who can write, since he belongs to the picturesque class of our great Baronet whose book you fostered. Osbert [Sitwell] is laid up at present in his ancestral halls with gout, his ancestral ailment, and his *Sing High, Sing Low* is not yet published here. His fame is extending over the Middle East, however, translations from his writings being published in Arabic, Persian, Demotic Greek and Russian and, as a friend of mine writes from Persia, "There has been nothing like it since Catherine the Great had the *Rambler* translated into the Russian and Osbert can boast, with Dr. Johnson, that he is being read on the banks of the Volga."

[1] Robert Gathorne-Hardy was the son of the 3rd Earl of Cranbrook. Educated at Eton and Oxford, he studied medicine and took a degree in law, but literature was closest to his heart. In 1928, when he was twenty-six, he met Smith and they were close friends for the next seventeen years. He wrote two well-known books on botany, *Wild Flowers in Britain* (1938) and *Garden Flowers* (1948), a book of poetry, and three novels, in addition to his *Recollections of Logan Pearsall Smith*.

The Younger Writers

TO EDWARD WEEKS   December 14, 1945

Of younger writers there are two you might keep your eye on, the ablest of whom, in my opinion (and Cyril's also) is Major Hugh Trevor-Roper (aged 32) a very distinguished Oxford scholar, who has been serving in a high post in the British Secret Service, and is now returning to Oxford to lead the life of an historian and writer.

What interests me is that he can write, and has, like Cyril, real fire in his belly. Perhaps you can judge his quality by the article on Hobbes which I enclose — not that I suppose you will want to print it, but you might be interested to see a sample from the book of Seventeenth century portraits he has promised me to write. His address is Christ Church, Oxford.

The second youth I have spotted is a certain young John Russell, who is a most accomplished journalist, but I think will turn out a fine critic as well. Cyril agrees with this. He certainly can write and I send you two of his articles to look at. He has just married a young Countess Apponyi, a dispossessed Hungarian aristocrat, and they have come to live in more than Hungarian poverty in rooms almost next door to me. (No. 15 St. Leonard's Terrace, S.W. 3.)

P.S. In my survey I quite forgot two items which are the most interesting of all:

1. The most gifted and promising of all Cyril Connolly's contemporaries is Sir Kenneth Clark, of whom you must have heard. Some fifteen years ago he was the favorite pupil of my brother-in-law Bernard Berenson, and it was his determination to follow in Berenson's footsteps and become his successor as the leading writer in Europe on the history of painting.

But after years of this apprenticeship the world got hold of him: good-looking, popular and absurdly rich, he was welcomed in the highest world of England, even by Royalty itself, and was pushed almost by force up the broad stairway of honor and power. At the incredibly early age of thirty he reached its highest peak, being made director of the National Gallery and created K. C. B. — the highest public honor next the Garter [an exaggeration].

And now he has grown sick of it all, is resigning the National Gallery, and has refused to accept the directorship of the British Council, the highest and most highly paid of all possible positions. He wants to return to his early ideal, and has promised me (we have always remained great friends) to present me on my next birthday with the great shining book (like Ruskin's *Modern Painters*) which I have always told him he has inside him. Keep your eye open for this.

2. Case two is even more interesting — indeed as far as I know unique in the history of literature, that of a poet finding his gift after the age of seventy. This poet (and he is a genuine poet) is also rich, and comes from a famous family. He is Robert Trevelyan, son of Sir George Trevelyan (the famous biographer of his uncle Lord Macaulay) and brother of George Trevelyan, the historian and the Master of Trinity College, Cambridge. Robert has written poetry all his life, but it was scholarly, muffled, and not in a voice and style authentically his own. But now he is enjoying a St. Martin's Summer, and all good judges regard the fruit of this late harvest as a real contribution to English literature. I send you herewith a specimen, on the haunting quality of which I stake my judgment, as I did on *The Burning of the Leaves* by Laurence Binyon. It has just been privately printed. If you with to print it, write to Robert Trevelyan, The Shiffolds, Holmbury St. Mary, Surrey.

* * *

TO EDWARD WEEKS

11 St. Leonard's Terrace
February 1, 1946

I wrote to you a little time ago to say that I was sending you a copy of *Orion,* which contains an essay of mine on my correspondence with Virginia Woolf.

You will notice [her] statement that the inheritance of great beauty had been a misfortune to her family. By means of it they married into great families much above their position.

[154]

For example her great-aunt Virginia Pattle had married Earl
Somers. The steel-trap Countess succeeded in marrying her
eldest daughter, the heiress to the Somers fortunes, to the
heir presumptive of the Duke of Beaufort (the eldest son
being considered unmarriageable). She went to live at Badminton, but her husband deigned to spend only one night
with her; from this encounter issued Somers Somerset, who
died not long ago. The rest of her life was what is now called
a sex-starved one. Finally she pried open a box in which she
found a romantic correspondence between Lord Henry and
a friend named M—— S—— [one of his footmen]. On
writing to her mother she gave an account of this incident,
whereupon the Countess, a woman of dramatic temperament,
arrived at Badminton at midnight, snatched Lady Henry
from her bed and escaped with her, clad only in a nightdress
and a waterproof, with one slipper on her foot and the other
in her hand, and carrying her infant son with her. In this
last step she broke the law, as it then was. Lord Henry
brought an action against her for the abduction of his son.
All England shook with the scandal, and the Judge, after
examining the contents of the box, declared Lady Henry
to have been perfectly justified in leaving, and in taking her
child with her. The family lawyers on both sides met to
discuss the position and finally decided that it would be best
settled if Lord Henry would accept 4,000 Pounds a year
from his wife, on condition that he lived permanently abroad.
He went to reside in Florence and entertained there almost
regally. After drunken debauches he and his pot-companions
used to urinate on a large bust of his wife, and otherwise
defile it. Lady Henry meanwhile became my mother's most
intimate friend, and by her was induced to take up temperance work. She discovered in herself an extraordinary gift,
which held great audiences spell-bound throughout England
and America. I knew her, as a boy, as a coarse-grained,
broad-bottomed old lady who kept us in a roar with accounts
of life at Badminton. "Pooh!" she would say, "You middle-
class people think yourselves snobbish and vulgar, but you
don't know what snobbery and vulgarity are, until you have
lived in a ducal household, where the Duke and Duchess sit

all day long singing to themselves in a soft undersong 'I'm a Duke, I'm a Duchess, I'm a Duchess, I'm a Duke,' and regarding the rest of the world as dirt."

All this I wrote to Sir Osbert [Sitwell], who is a descendant of the Beauforts — a close clan who would prefer these striking incidents to be buried beneath the dust of oblivion; and he has written to ask me not to include them in my life of my mother. This seems to me rather like Satan rebuking sin, considering his own revelations about his ancestors, but I am fond of him and have promised to submit any relevant passages to him. His sister Miss Edith Sitwell has also written to say that middle-class people cannot understand the semi-princely ways of the descendents of the Plantagenets; I have replied that my point of view may be that of the middle class, but that its value as a standard of honorable conduct is better discussed with Osbert than with herself.

All this would have made an interesting amendment to my article; but some people seemed to have liked it as it was printed, for it was highly praised by the critics, as you may judge from the article by Desmond MacCarthy which I enclose; so if you care to print it, I shan't mind in the least.

Speaking of Miss Edith Sitwell, I enclose herewith her latest volume of poems. When I happened to come across the lines which begin

> I who was once a golden woman like those who walk
> In the dark heavens — but am now grown old
> And sit by the fire, and see the fire grow cold . . .

I said "Hullo, this is poetry," the old gift of incantatory poetry which I thought had ceased. No other living poet could have written these magical lines. I read on with interest and astonishment and was much impressed by the beauty and strangeness of this maiden lady's musical cater-waulings. When I mentioned her to my friends, I found that they all took her greatness for granted. Rose Macaulay tells me, in fact, that there is a strong movement on foot to make her Poet Laureate, when old Masefield feebly but finally kicks the bucket. Only yesterday Cyril Connolly told me that he too was in the movement. Miss Sitwell tells me that she was vilely treated by Macmillan in New York, and I do think that American publishers should be interested in this new wild incantatory music. You have Miss Sitwell's permission to do anything you like with her poems, and I hope that at any rate you will read them.

A little time ago I sent you some specimens of other authors' work. Since then I have heard that my brother-in-law Berenson has written the diary of his adventures while hiding in the mountains under an assumed name during the German occupation of Tuscany. People think highly of it; I don't myself think highly of his gift for writing, but I think the subject-matter may be of interest. By some miracle he remained safely hid in the mountains, while his German secretary and wife pretended that the villa, library and collection of pictures were theirs, and therefore German property. Though up to 100 German soldiers were billeted there, the property was protected by large signs saying "German property — not to be disturbed." Göring made three attempts to find Berenson's library and pictures, but could find no trace of them. When the Germans left, B.B. emerged from his hiding place and returned to find, among the ruins, his own habitation completely unharmed. As I haven't read the journal I can't vouch for it personally, but it might be worth your while to get hold of it.[1] If you are interested you should write to him direct.

[1] This was published as *Rumor and Reflection* in 1952 by Simon and Schuster, New York.

Public Affairs

What to Do with the Jews

This letter survived among Smith's papers without full identification. It was unsigned but the style is unmistakably his and the subject is one about which he obviously felt very deeply.

Sir,   April 16, 1938

It seems to be generally admitted that those who are now governing the world are unfitted for the task; that our civilization is rapidly disintegrating, and that we are confronted by two horrors, Nazism and Communism of which it would be difficult to say which presents the more ghastly prospect.

The first symptom of this disintegration is almost everywhere in persecution of the Jews. But what purpose is gained by beating and banning the most intelligent, most cultivated and cosmopolitan race of Europe? The Jews are lovers of the countries in which they are born, and too few to attempt the conquest of any other, and their territorial claims are so minute as to be ridiculous. They are not lovers of bloodshed or propagandists of any religion; without their patronage painting and music would collapse in almost every city of Europe and America; the Jews are the best doctors and scientists in the world, and three of them, Marx, Freud and Einstein, have made the most brilliant contributions to modern thought. Europe also derives its religion from them since the Virgin Mary, Christ and all the apostles were Jews. Like the rest of us they have their faults, and are supposed to be fonder of money than we are. But a twentieth part of what we are now spending on armaments would satisfy them, and leave enough over to transport, say to Central Australia, those who don't like them, with an ample supply of bombs with which to exterminate each other.

The Greeks committed suicide by their internecine hatreds. Why should we, their Aryan inheritors, commit the same ghastly error? We maintain that we possess, what the Greeks did not, a revelation from Heaven, in which God plainly declares that he has chosen the Jews to govern the world. We are universally taught that one of them did actually save it. I don't happen to believe this, and I haven't a drop of Jewish blood in my veins. But in the meantime, I should like to see Jews like the late Lord Reading govern the world, and I think they might possibly save it. For the Jews do love civilization, and the liberty of which it is the flower; and I happen to love them too.

War Days

London Bombed

11 St. Leonard's Terrace

TO ROBERT GATHORNE-HARDY August 28, 1939

War seems almost certain. Most of my friends are fleeing from London, but I shall stay here, and be bombed if heaven wishes it. There is nowhere I want to go and my life is practically over anyhow.

* * *

TO HUGH TREVOR-ROPER March 21, 1941

I find, I must confess, an apocalyptic splendor in the blitzes, with the roar of their artillery, their fiery chariots and flaring lights. They seem like great rehearsals of the great Day of Judgment. I love standing on my doorstep and gazing with joy and fear at the spectacle. Just enough fear to make it pleasant; I do not expect any resurrection for the Great Assize and if my house blazes up and I am consumed in a bonfire of old bones, I shall not greatly care. But before that trivial catastrophe I shall hope to see you if only to be given back some books. Whether you come as a friend or as a hyena you will be welcome. A combination of the two would be what would suit me best.

* * *

I suppose that you are, like all your compatriots (if patriot is the word) off on Whitsun holidays and won't be back for some weeks. I am left alone to face the Germans and am pilloried at the Town Hall as the laugh of Chelsea since, poor mug that I am, I was taken in by the propaganda echoing on the loudspeakers through the streets about the deadly peril of my adopted country and its need for arms. So, out of my depleted purse I sent a donation which has proved to be double that of any other inhabitant of this opulent borough, to the War Weapons Week's fund and am held up to the derision I deserve.

The consequences of this is that, as you have no doubt already observed (if you have read this letter) the old American eagle has begun squawking in my breast; I thought I had wrung the neck of that tiresome fowl fifty years ago! But the smug complacency and sunshine talk of all the people I meet, and above all, the asinine broadcasts of Duff Cooper, have "got my goat" and I am venting my spleen on you. I want to warn you too that other hyenas have begun to haunt my house, so my bookshelves will soon be empty. Rose Macaulay has lost everything through enemy action, as we call it: clothes, manuscripts, all her books; she faces the world with only a pot of marmalade and the clothes she stands in, trying to decide in what new character she shall begin life again. She says she is too old to be a street walker, too patriotic to be a spy, too poor to set up as a Mayfair Jezebel. I have suggested social climbing, not in Hill Street, or Mayfair, but on less-frequented peaks, Denmark Hill or Muswell Hill, or even Notting Hill. Are there any peaks in your neighborhood that no one has yet climbed?

*　*　*

We have had our windows broken, but otherwise are unbloody, though not unbowed. We fall on our knees when the bombs scream over Chelsea, but our nights are quiet. *Primus in orbe deos fecit Timor.* I repeat this line of Statius as I note what seems to be the beginnings of a religious revival in this bombed city.

I've read the book you recommended — Paget's *Paradoxes and Puzzles* — what a show-up of that old Whig scoundrel Macaulay!

*　*　*

TO HUGH TREVOR-ROPER   January 5, 1945

I much enjoyed our joyride yesterday and hope it amused you. After being so nearly snuffed out in the morning of Wednesday [by an air bombing] I tasted the pleasure of survival, and of good company on Thursday. No doubt

> "There's much to be said
> for being dead"

and something may be said for being alive, also; especially if one takes life (as one had better take it) in a picaresque fashion. Seen in any other way it's really too absurd.

Old Age

Growing old is no gradual decline, but a series of tumbles, full of sorrow, from one ledge to another. Yet when we pick ourselves up we find that our bones are not broken; while not unpleasing is the new terrace which lies unexplored before us.

— *Last Words*

On the Death of His Mother

Hannah Whitall Smith died at Oxford on May 1, 1911, after suffering a stroke three days earlier. She was seventy-nine years old.

TO LADY OTTOLINE MORRELL

Iffley, Oxford
May 3, 1911

Thank you so much for your dear kind letter and thought of my mother. She died not long after I wrote to you, and her message to you was almost the last time she spoke. She asked us what the doctor had said and when I told her that she was worse, her eyes brightened and she said "Good!" Then she fell quietly asleep, her breathing grew less and less and then ceased with a little sigh. It was inexpressibly tranquil and beautiful; the fulfillment of a long and noble life in perfect peace, her papers and books about her, and the sunshine and flowers and birds that she loved to watch just outside her window. Death, if it can be like that, need have no terrors, and it was so exactly what she had long wished that it seems selfish to mourn over it, as we cannot help mourning. She so dreaded, poor dear, any failure of mind or increased infirmity, lest she should become a burden to us or sadden our lives in any way, and she had long prayed that she might die just like this. We longed to keep her with us a few more years but she has had her wish, and we must not grieve too much. I cannot tell you how sad and beautiful the thought of it all is — she really was perfectly generous and absolutely unselfish, wise, serene, courageous — none of us ever had a quarrel about anything with her — her love for us and her trust in God were so perfect that she never let our differences of views or anything we did trouble her — or if they did, she never by the slightest sign let us know it; and if we had all gone away and neglected her in her old age, she never would have said a word, or even have blamed us in her thoughts. It really is wonderful to know that poor querulous human nature can now and then flower with characters like hers, without selfishness or meanness, or pettiness of any kind — a person of passionate feelings and impulses, but governed by a perfectly-fashioned will, growing old and wise in years and experience, making mistakes perhaps, but never repeating them, and learning more and more from life, instead of being made querulous or peevish by it. What an enormous, quite immeasurable difference after all, goodness does make, and how beautiful it is beyond any other beauty. One saw it bringing its rewards to her in those last years of her ripe old age — her cheerfulness in spite of her infirmities, her gayety of spirits, her secret joy in the thought of approaching death, the wealth of love that surrounded her, the letters that came to her almost every day, from all over the world, telling her of the gratitude and affection of the unknown friends her books had made for her — and she now goes bearing her sheaves with her, either to perfect rest, or, as we must hope, to the God she loved so passionately.

Her poor body is to be burned tomorrow, as she wished, with just the family present.

Appreciating the Calm

11 St. Leonard's Terrace

TO HIS SISTER MARY   February 2, 1925

I am most distressed about Alys [who had been ill while visiting at I Tatti] and feel deep sympathy with all your woes. What a frail raft we float upon on the so-called sea of life, and what monsters swim in it, ready to gobble us up — and certain to do so in the end. We ought to learn to appreciate and enjoy more than we do each interval of calm and sun- shine — and there are such intervals even at our age. Saint-Beuve says it is frivolous and unnatural to be well and happy to the end, — it is better to grow old in a manner more consonant with the common destiny of men. The best to be said for old age was that it was the only way which has yet been discovered for living a long time.

Loneliness and Solitude

Venice

TO CYRIL CONNOLLY   April 24, 1927

I am sorry that your woe has descended on you, but that is the price which you pay for your ecstasy, and it is a price which I am sure you are not unwilling to pay. Yours is a life of dizzy heights and deep abysses — I envy it in a way, for it is a life of that poignant reality which is the stuff of art; but my serene and pleased indifference, the "constant mood of my calm thoughts" suits best my temperament and my years. You are right in saying that I do not suffer from loneliness, and that I should regard any tie which made me feel it as a chain which bound me to the great wheel.

*   *   *

TO DESMOND MACCARTHY   June 6, 1927

I was much interested in your last Hawk [MacCarthy wrote in the *New Statesman* under the name Affable Hawk] about solitude. It is a problem and I don't think there is any solu- tion for it. Solitude makes one melancholy, but to taste life and its significance one must be alone.

The Inevitable Old Bore

TO JANE CLARK   June 25, 1935

I am of course growing old — a process much assisted by my
long illness last winter. I am quite conscious that I have
fallen into the stage of anecdotage, in which I like to tell
(and no doubt repeat) long stories about people and my own
experiences and recollections. I don't expect people to listen
to these (that would be asking too much) but I am grateful
if they will occasionally and for a few minutes pretend to
listen as I mumble on. I shall be grateful if you and K will
exercise this charity now and then. The realization that one
is regarded as an old bore is an inevitable incident, of course,
of one's declining years; but it isn't altogether pleasant; and as
we must all suffer it sooner or later, we should be charitable
to each other. I have no present grievance in writing this as
you have always both been most kind in lending me your
ears. I am only making (with the prosiness of my years) a
general observation on a matter which has been recently
forced upon my attention.

Looking Backward

11 St. Leonard's Terrace

TO KENNETH CLARK   October 5, 1936

I was glad to hear that you liked my essays on their reperusal
[Reperusals and Recollections]. It is certainly a satisfaction
when one is old — I shall be seventy-one next week — to
feel that I have done the best I could to develop my tiny
talent. This sense Henry James has described as the real
life of the artist, the absence of it as his death. He likes to
feel that he has drawn from his instrument the finest music
that nature has hidden in it, and has played it as it should
be played. My achievement seems to me paltry enough,
Heaven knows, but I doubt I could have done anything
better. Perhaps if I hadn't had any money? But after all
I did live on 300 Pounds a year until I was nearly fifty;

and when more money came to me later (most of it has now vanished in the American collapse) that poison came to me too late to do me any serious harm. I like money so as to be able to travel in the most comfortable fashion, otherwise I am more or less indifferent to it, save for a minimum of comfort, which costs really very little. I agree with Emerson that a rush of thoughts is the only conceivable prosperity that can come to us, and if 300,000 Pounds was offered to me on the condition that I should spend three months in America or Australia, I should turn down the offer without hesitation. But vanity seems to have got hold of my pen, which is a symptom no doubt of my unvenerable age.

I have followed your career with much interest and admiration and I find B.B. most enthusiastic about all you have done and are doing. Of course we both hoped that you would take to the life of the detached scholar and writer; I know that that sort of life had its temptations for you, but I think your decision was a wise one. Foxes without tails always want to see other foxes mutilate themselves in the same fashion; anyhow, the world never wanted us or made us any kind of offer. We had to sneak about, more or less despised and lonely and no young man full of life and blood and energy and the consciousness of great activities such as you possess, could have been happy in the meager despised sort of existence which was ours for many years. No one should adopt it save under the compulsion of a vocation so overpowering that there is no alternative and the question simply doesn't arise, as it never did for me. Of course with such a vocation a life dedicated to following it has many pleasures. The leisurely years are delicious years and one's old age is haunted by no regrets. Certainly my life has been an extraordinarily happy one. I can repeat to critics of it Santayana's question, "What riches have you that you deem me poor, Or what large comfort that you call me sad?"

I feel that I have lived in a Golden Age and now that it seems to be drawing to a disastrous end (as all Golden Ages do) I don't repine in the least at the prospect of leaving a world which seems to present no prospects but those of horror and disaster.

I hear you are going to America next week, so I don't
suppose there is any chance of seeing you before you go —
you must be frightfully busy.

Give my best love to Jane. I have been sorry to hear that
she hasn't been well. I hope she will soon be all right and
ready for the stupendous fray of your American adventure.
I can't think of anyone I would care to talk to in that vast
vociferous China of commonplace and platitude — yes, there
is my cousin, Mrs. Simon Flexner, who Roger [Fry] told me
was the most charming woman he had met in America. Her
husband Simon Flexner is the most distinguished American
bacteriologist and also a delightful talker. He has just retired
from the directorship of the great Rockefeller Institute.

The Permanent Invalid

11 St. Leonard's Terrace

TO EDWARD MARSH   December 28, 1936

I hope you will enjoy your declining years as much as I am
enjoying mine. Let me recommend the role that I have
adopted of the permanent invalid, which is a bit old-fashioned,
but which, since age and heart-feebleness, and what Henry
James called "the wear and tear of discrimination" has forced
it upon me, I find delightful. One can be as cantankerous as
one wants to be, think of nothing but one's own comforts.
One can see only the people one wants to see and get his
doctor to give orders that one must not be contradicted. So,
now I can say what I like — when I was well no one ever
listened to me.

From a Bench of Desolation

11 St. Leonard's Terrace

TO ROBERT GATHORNE-HARDY   May 28, 1940

I have been going over masses of old family papers, and renewing my memory of the past with old photographs and
letters. Here is a sentence from one of my mother's letters

written when she was about my present age — "I hope you enjoy as much as I do to see the earthly life beginning to fade away a little. It is so delicious to get done with this world, and to have the beautiful prospect of the next world draw nearer and nearer day by day." All but the last clause expresses what I am feeling — I do rather enjoy "seeing the earthly life beginning to fade a little." And yet it has never shone so prettily in my eyes as in its (presumed) fading in this sea of woe. [A reference to the war.] And I have charming adventures — a new bookshop has just been opened round the corner by one of the succession of foolish bookish youths who open bookshops in Chelsea, and then soon have to close them. I have just been there and have bought for 3d one of the rarest, and to my mind, the most delightful of Henry James' books, *Terminations*.

I sit out in the gardens opposite every afternoon. Do you remember the gaunt, aristocratic spinster murderess we talked with there one afternoon? As you know, I have that delicious so-called affliction of age, that softening of the brain which makes everything I write and say seem delicious; so that, as we sit on what Desmond [MacCarthy] calls my "bench of desolation," I can tell over and over to the spinster my favorite stories, and enjoy them more and more each time I tell them, while she who is suffering, she says, from the same loss of memory, declares that they are all perfectly new and fresh to her each time I tell them. So there we sit telling each other stories of old scandal, each sunny afternoon.

Waiting

11 St. Leonard's Terrace

TO ROBERT GATHORNE-HARDY   June 13, 1940

I am so sorry to hear of Kyrle's [Kyrle Leng] illness. Give him my love. We are all probably doomed creatures, seated on volcanoes that may burst into flame at any moment; or are floating, shipwrecked, on rafts amid stormy seas. All we can do is to shout vain words, or wave wan white towels or handkerchiefs to each other in the distance. No, that isn't the full truth, since I at least do other things, leading a quite pleasant existence; polishing phrases as I lie in bed in the morning, or watching charming youths play cricket or tennis all the afternoon. Above them floats the silvery crescent of the new moon, looking inconceivably icy and remote and lovely and unconcerned, as I gaze at it through my field glasses, floating in the azure sky above me, a picture of the serene desolation which is the ultimate fate of this bloody planet.

History: Living and Reading

11 St. Leonard's Terrace

TO HUGH TREVOR-ROPER   March 21, 1941

I wonder if you are still alive and back in Barnet.[1] If so, I hope you will pay me a visit one of these days. I am still alive, at least people say so.

I greatly enjoy your visits, though being old and full up to the lips with disillusion, I can't quite make out whether you have sneaked into my life as a hyena to filch my books, or have come from Heaven to befriend a bosom much bereaved by the dirty vanishing trick commonly called by the august name of Death. They are all gone, I echo after Lamb, "the old familiar faces" — the derision of dear Walter Raleigh, the malicious pity of Henry James, who used to raise his hands to Heaven and murmur, "Poor Logan, poor Logan!" and the grave disapproval of Robert Bridges. As to the still graver face of that primitive hildago Santayana, I shall never see it again. To quote you Shakespeare's lines

> "Thy bosom is endeared with all hearts,
> Which I by lacking have supposed dead"[2]

would be a height of sentiment which would not be welcome from a half-witted old derelict like me.

You must have perceived that I am touched in the brain, a candidate for Bedlam. My deviations from the normal are various, some pleasant, some distressing. The worst of these are of a manic-depressive nature. I spend, like Persephone, half the year in dull regions beneath the earth. All last winter

[170]

I hibernated and was only half alive; now with the spring I have emerged into light again; but like the infant of Saguntum[3] who poked his head out of his mother's womb when that city was being sacked and not liking what he saw, returned to the warm security he was leaving. I don't like the look of things which present themselves to my eyes. Yet am I being honest? Isn't it interesting not only to read history (I read all day long) but to live through it?

[1] A London suburb where certain intelligence offices of the Army were located.
[2] Sonnet XXXI.
[3] See page 75.

The Aims of Life

TO HUGH TREVOR-ROPER

11 St. Leonard's Terrace
June 26, 1941

Many thanks for your letter which pleased me greatly. The young seldom realize, I think, how much pleasure they give by their company or letters to older derelicts who have few friends remaining to listen to their divagations. You do listen to my moralizings and my memories, and though your eye wanders around my bookshelves, I find comfort in the thought that you seem to find your demands satisfied with books when with other young visitors my store of banknotes is often depleted before they leave. But this is only an accidental explanation of my pleasure in your conversation for I liked you before I saw you, feeling from a certain tang in your use of words that you really were aware of the Platonic truth that words and phrases are the only things that matter; and that objects and actions are only gross and awkward and empty shadows of their meaning. These latter objects, with your laudable love of the world and the flesh and the devil, you will no doubt pursue and break your heart in the process. Unless indeed I can save you — or what is much the same thing — ruin your life by my example and preaching. Up from my Chelsea garret there reaches a Jacob's ladder to Heaven and down below a Capri cliff and the street where an ambulance is always waiting. Which course my visitors take is always a matter of kindly sympathy to me; it is only when they slip down the drain that I lose interest in them.

But I see that I am trying to make myself out a remarkable person, when I am really only a malicious old moralist whose humor is, while waiting for the next blackmailer, to preach a sermon on life and its conduct — a sermon to which, I daresay, you won't bother to listen.

Health, wealth, and happiness, I begin prosaically, are supposed to be the reasonable aims of life, instead of your world, flesh, and the devil. On the whole I accept this prosaic view, though here I think certain distinctions and discriminations may be useful. *Health* certainly I should put first among all human goods, and *wealth,* if limited to the supply of financial independence, is a most important ingredient in good fortune. But money suffers from the law of diminishing returns — a little is of immense importance but any nimiety or too much brings with it sorrow. My view on this point is probably a perverted one that the mass of mankind would think unnatural; but I have been both poor and rich and lived a great part of my life with rich people who almost always suffer from boredom, and are bores themselves in consequence. They have to live in a kind of leper house together; the companionship of the clever rich with the interesting poor is impossible; too unjust; the poor knowing that the rich could, with a few strokes of the pen, relieve them of their dreadful troubles, don't realize that the rich have learned from bitter experience that the fruit of such kindness is almost always ingratitude and envy. *Wealth* therefore I place among the cups of poison; it spoils the happiness of the inheritors, drives down the drain those who crave it, into the sink of profitable publicity and shoddy writing into which almost all the young people of promise I have tried to encourage have disappeared beyond my cognizance — though not beyond my pity.

To prove, however, that I am not quite the prig I seem, I will admit a weakness for one cup of poison, that of social success, whose flavor, as far as I have tasted it, is delicious and which I have never known anyone resist to whom it has been proffered. *Power* is, I believe, even more poisonous and more delicious, but that I have never tasted so I stick to my conviction that the real secret of happiness is not holiness nor goodness but a vocation — some disinterested job, say that of painting, or, like mine, of polishing phrases, which one can work at all one's life and never get tired for a moment.

A Feeling for Words

11 St. Leonard's Terrace

TO HUGH TREVOR-ROPER   September 29, 1942

You were so kind to the old derelict I feel myself to be last Sunday, listened so patiently to his divagations that I feel I must thank you for the friendly way you treat me. As I told you, I think, I enjoy your company more than that of anyone now living; and in it I enjoy what Emerson said was the best thing in life, the "perfect understanding between sincere people." This felt harmony of life with life, these unanimous thoughts, as Santayana calls them, shared allegiances and execrations, are limited, of course. Friends, he warns us, can only be friends in spots. But these bright spots are precious and I find more of them with you than with anyone. Of course there are black spots in me that you don't like, and I find blind, if not black, ones in you. One of these, by the way, is your lack of interest in the philosopher whom I have been quoting and whom I regard as the most important person now living — which after all is not saying very much. Another blindness which I thought I detected in you was one which envelops all your generation, a blindness to the glory of words. I showed you my test book of starry epithets and seemed to see you look at it with glazed, or at least with cold eyes, and felt that the word-fancier whom I am looking for in vain through the world has not and would never now make an appearance. But I felt differently when I saw you anxious to open my *Oxford Dictionary* and learned that you read our Society for Pure English pamphlets. My dictionaries must be yours, I felt, and my choice philological library, when I fade away into the azure. So, I am arranging a visit this week to my solicitor to make these and other arrangements.

Bob Trevelyan has just arrived. He has rented the room in this house which for thirty years was his for nothing. But as he has inherited a great fortune, while my investments now pay the most exiguous dividends, the rent of his room will help to pay the rent on this house, which will be useful. Besides, I find his conversation pleasant.

Some Lingering Questions

TO HUGH TREVOR-ROPER

11 St. Leonard's Terrace
October 20, 1942

I did happen to read your note which reached me this morning and I much appreciate your kindness and tact in remembering my birthday . . . My life has been, as you must have guessed, one of prolonged and scrupulous introspection. On the whole it has been a pleasant process — and lucrative, I may boast, as well. But now and then I come on phenomena which I find difficult of explanation . . .

1. Where was Melchisedek during the Flood which he survived? (St. Augustine, I read, was haunted all his life by this problem.)

2. Did David's father commit adultery when he begat the Psalmist on his legitimate wife but believed (as many hold) that he was embracing her handmaid?

3. What was the cause of Ovid's exile? Did he catch Augustus committing incest or something worse, as Voltaire suggests in the phrase *torra tuentibus hircis?*[1]

Such are the problems by which I am preoccupied in the grave meditations suitable to my venerable years.

By the way, I don't want to cross that threshold leaving you under the misapprehension that there are only six sexes. I was right when I said there were eight: I had merely forgotten the two bi-sexual sexes, though I am told that they are to be met everywhere today.

[174]

So you see I have grave moral information to impart, as well as what you maliciously call "malicious gossip," which isn't really gossip at all, for no one hates gossip more than I do. It's what should be called "facing life," which is the duty of us all. Or at its worst, it is with me nothing but the gilding of the pill of the moral instruction which the venerable owe to the young. But to avoid misunderstanding, when you come again (which I hope will be soon) I shall discourse on nothing but the True, the Beautiful, and the Good.

[1] The correct quotation should be *Transversa tuentibus hircis* ("with the goats looking askance") from Virgil, *Eclogue* 3, line 8.

On Flattery

11 St. Leonard's Terrace

TO HUGH TREVOR-ROPER   October 20, 1942

I must thank you for your kind thought of me on my birthday — or pretended birthday, for one birthday we can only have, unless indeed we are reborn (and my prospects for that still more comical regeneration are not worth betting on, not more than sixpence anyway). But as an occasion for a birthday present from you, the date is certainly welcome. Of the three dainty tributes you suggest, Sallust is my choice. I am afraid of a book on hunting; such books are apt to cause me dreams, not the delicious dreams you indelicately refer to (I am past the time when those glimpses of heaven beglamor the sleep though they soil the bedclothes of the Saints) but of misbehavior on the hunting field, running over the hounds, being publicly rebuked by the M.F.H., etc. etc.

If I might be greedy (and why not be greedy?) I should like also the little flattering dish you hint at. My love for flattery has not escaped your acute observation and the thrill of transparency that I experience when your gaze is fixed upon me is one which, I imagine, must make translucent vases vibrate with pleasure. For to be seen through and yet tolerated, not to be detested and smashed to pieces — no self-exhibiting old clergyman can taste an ecstasy like this with the police around the corner. But with your all-piercing vision you must have observed that though no flattery is unwelcome, the breath and faint garlic of derision in the salads you prepare, the drops (I won't say of poison) of not unfriendly irony you infuse in your sauces, is especially to my taste and I am always grateful for it.

But my gratitude to you, you must have seen (as you see everything) shining with almost too bright a glow. I won't let it scorch my paper as you already know how much I enjoy your company and conversation and the admiration (just pleasantly touched with fear) which I feel for your gifts of mind and character.

Speaking of Saints, rumor has no doubt reached you of the miracles which St. Rose[1] of Hinde Street has taken to performing: she restores the sight of the blind, cures women with issues (whatever that may be), and casts out devils. She refuses, however, to cast out the spirit of uncleanness which, as you have often told me, has taken possession of me. She enjoys, she says, its bawdy badinage. But she is coming to a birthday luncheon which Paul Sudley is giving me on Thursday (we are both quite willing to accept the hospitality of the heirs of Earls) and as our host has, he says, no alcoholic potations, she has promised to turn his Lordship's water into wine. We have only to name the vintage. What would you suggest? A Quaker like myself and an ex-Presbyterian like St. Rose would not know what to choose. . . .

To end my garrulous letter with a moral (as becomes a sage writing to a stripling) I will tell you the sad, instructive tale of my friend Bob Trevelyan, whom I am going to visit this afternoon at Westminster Hospital. Having been lucky enough to retain, beyond the Psalmist's limit, the charming gift of infatuation, he has been long in the habit of spending one night a week in the room above my bedroom, in order to take out to dinner the Princess (almost always middle-aged and dowdy) of his changing affections. Last Friday he arrived as usual, but had not, as usual, returned at midnight. I hoped that he hadn't received a rebuff, as usually happens, but was spending the night in the arms of his beloved. But at 1 o'clock

[176]

St. George's hospital rang up to say that he had been picked up unconscious in the street, having been bumped in the blackout by a bus or other vehicle. He was removed in a dangerous condition to Westminster, where, as he is now out of danger, I shall be allowed to see him for a few minutes this afternoon.

¹ Rose Macaulay.

Age or Youth?

11 St. Leonard's Terrace
TO LIEUTENANT J. W. LAMBERT   November 2, 1942

I much enjoyed your letter, and whatever rank you illustrate you must certainly be given a high place among the English letter-writers — with FitzGerald, shall we say, and Cowper and Lamb and Horace Walpole — somewhere among these, but high enough to make me desire your company as well as your correspondence. I will therefore accept with alacrity your offer to make me your brother officer on the *Mantis* — I agree with you that this would be better than coming as a common rating, though my wants are simple. All I need really is a Vi-spring bed, in which my breakfast can be served not later than 9:30 (for I am an early riser), a second cabin containing the Oxford Dictionary (18 vols), the Dialect Dictionary (6 vols), 27 other books of reference, and an unlimited supply of writing paper on which to write my impressions and meditations. I shall need a bathroom of my own and a cabin too for a servant who looks after my health and comfort — an elderly ex-lady's maid, who has lived in the best houses and knows exactly how things should be done, hot water bottles filled, and cushions and pillows and bedclothes arranged. She, like me, has come down in the world; but our demands are very simple, and we shall be glad to be doing our bit for our King and country. It may be thought that I am rather too old for Naval service, but I am not much more than fifty years older than you are, and have been much longer at sea. I used to spend all my summers yachting. Besides sailing my own yacht, I would go for a cruise every year with a Baronet and member of the Royal Yacht Squadron. So I am used to sailing under the

White Ensign; and although the meaning of the word *Snob* is quite beyond my comprehension, and I regard all worldly glories and distinctions as piffle before the wind, I confess I do taste a mild exhilaration in sailing out of harbors on the Solent beneath the white emblem, when all the other yachts display blue or red flags, and burgees that make one blush to look at them. But I am a very simple and modest person; and if delicate allusions occur now and then concerning the merits of my writings, and arrangements are made for my fan letters to reach me promptly, you and your fellow-officers will, I think, find me pleasant company on the *Mantis.* In preparation for my embarkment on this tiny vessel, I have been looking up the "Tiger of the Insect World," whose name your motor-boat bears. The Arabs believe that the Mantis always prays with its face towards Mecca; it is honored among the Nubians, and the Chinese keep it in bamboo boxes, and match it in cockfights, in which it unsheaths its raptorial and rapier-like wings to destroy its adversary in dreadful conflicts. But the female Mantis is still more fierce, and when the male returns from victory to her embraces, she eats it up at once. That you will never meet with such harsh treatment from the lady who is the mother of your son, I wish sincerely, and would like to send my compliments and congratulations not only to the father, but to the mother of this new arrival.

As to what the world into which you have projected this infant will be like, I cannot send news that will be altogether reassuring. Whether it be dominated by Beaverbrook, by Hitler, Stalin, Japan or America, I am rather glad I shall not live to see; and if you drop me overboard, suitably swathed, from the decks of the *Mantis,* I shall sink beneath the waves with no exaggerated sorrow. The world I lived in for 77 years was a golden one; I enjoyed it to the limit of enjoyment. But Golden Ages have their sunsets, and then the darkness falls.

But of all this we will talk on the deck of the *Mantis,* beneath the winter stars.

> An old age, serene and bright,
> And lovely as a Lapland night

shall lead me to my watery grave. You will, following Biblical advice, rejoice in your youth (Proverbs, xi, 9). Which is the better state, age or youth, the Gods alone know, as Socrates would have put it.

Birthday Presents: A Reversal

TO HUGH TREVOR-ROPER

11 St. Leonard's Terrace
November 4, 1942

It would touch your heart (if you have such an organ — a question still open to doubt, in my opinion) it would touch your heart if I told you the sad story of my 78th birthday. It was a fiasco. Paul Sudley discussed with me the project of a birthday luncheon; but when he found that I thought he was going to provide the viands, instead of me, he sent a telephone message to say that he was going to the country on sudden business. I find that all my friends expect me to give *them* birthday presents on my own birthday, and are huffed at not receiving any, as you seem to be huffed, since I have heard nothing of you lately. So, instead of sending me the Sallust you promised and the delicately poisoned dish of flattery there was talk of, you seem to have dropped my acquaintance. So, therefore, to prevent this rupture (which would grieve *me*) I tottered out yesterday to a distant distinguished bookshop which as a rule only caters for the inhabitants of the stately homes of England (I and Maurice Baring are perhaps the only exceptions) and ordered in that shabby, dim, remote, exclusive shop an exquisite present for you, a volume of perhaps the most distinguished and exquisite English prose published in this century, of which I am pretty sure you have never even heard the title mentioned, such is the set of Philistines in which you quaff your liquor.

But though I distribute birthday presents on my birthdays (thus adopting the new custom of your disobliging generation) I keep my old disability to do up parcels, so if you want your birthday gift you must fetch it yourself.

p.s. In hinting at the dearth of presents on my birthday, I ought to have made an exception. The English Rose sent me a

[179]

charming one but *she* is a real Saint, not a bogus one from
Barnet. Only like all converts she is rather overdoing her
conversion and putting on a halo that does not become her. I
rang up her telephone number yesterday three times but each
time was answered by a deep bass voice of a he-man. She had
apparently performed a miracle unknown so far in the
Christian church and changed her sex, like Tiresias who was
blinded, as you remember, by Hera for saying that, having
been both a man and a woman, she knew that women
derived more pleasure than men from the well-known act of
copulation.

P.S. St. Rose of Hinde Street W.I., has just rung me up to say
that, finding Tiresias was right, she has resumed her sex and
is once more a lady.

Turning the Other Cheek

11 St. Leonard's Terrace
November 8, 1942

TO HUGH TREVOR-ROPER

When a bulky envelope was brought to me yesterday by my
dragon and I saw on it your always most welcome writing, my
mouth watered; I smacked my lips at the thought infinitely
more pleasant than that of the coffee, the toast and egg the
dragon also brought me, of the exquisite, long-promised dish,
the laurel salad, so to speak, on which I fondly hoped to
breakfast. What a dainty dish it will be, I gobbled; there will
be myrtle from Parnassus, fragrant herbs from the slopes of
Helicon, drops of Aeonian dew; and in the sauce of that
kindly liquor, just a drop of that astringent poison which will
keep the dish from being fulsome. After all my 78 years of
crying alone in the wilderness, my voice has found a friendly
echo, there is such a thing, I said to myself, as friendship in
the world!

You can guess then how my jaws fell when I found the
poison there all right but no taste or touch of any of the in-
gredients that should sweeten the dish — no myrtle or laurel,
or candied fruits of kindness, nothing but insults and insinua-
tions and scurrilous abuse, and the intimation of some awful

mud-bath of bad taste that once on a time I had wallowed in. I deny the merd you fling at me from your mudraking; never has my white garment of good taste been soiled or sullied in this manner. And this from one who has blasphemed Virgil as you have blasphemed him! How I shall rejoice at the Day of Judgment when I hear you sentenced to roast in the seats of the reprobates and doomed to dwell with devils to eternal ages!

But I will not retaliate; I will practice on you the dirty trick which Christ invented; I will turn the other cheek. No, (following the advice of a Chinese saint, whose spirit was more mild even than that of Jesus) I won't even wipe away from my cheek the gob of venom you have spat upon it. To do so, the Chinese saint suggested, might hurt the spitter's feelings. On the contrary, confessing my unworthiness, I will humbly try to help you in your search, hitherto in vain, for the promised dish of praise.

1. Several people, on reading my article in the *Observer* [on Max Beerbohm's seventieth birthday] have observed that at the age of seventy-seven I can write better than I ever wrote before. This observation I like.

2. It has been said of me that although I am beneath contempt myself, I nevertheless have nice friends. As you are the latest and (at present) the most highly appreciated addition to this distinguished body, you are almost compelled to repeat this praise.

3. People have also said that I have never recommended them to read anything really second-rate. This is what I like to hear more than anything.

4. That you like my bawdy conversation, you cannot say; and now that I have heard from clerical sources the explanation of this insipidity and aridity of your mind and temperament, I can pity and forgive it, and will not defile your mind with the feast of low-down I battened on yesterday when I lunched at the Atheneum with some fruity members of that club who were anxious to know in what way the Baronet was wicked, whose portrait adorns the current number of *Horizon*. Following, as always, your instructions, I am collecting quite a lot of these self-portraits. Yours comes next in merit to that of the lascivious Baronet, everyone agrees to that; but to miti-

gate the Miltonic austerity of this grim portrait ("O, flesh, flesh, how art thou fishified!" as Mercutio said most justly to the romantic Romeo) whereas, to quote again the Swan of Avon, don't you, as Launcelot said of old Gobbo "something smack, something grow to, have a kind of taste" — Well, to put it baldly, isn't your nose becoming slightly purple over your potations? It's a compensation, they say, for what makes a line of Southey's being not inapplicable to you — his famous line about the fish which he describes as

"Legless, unloving, infamously chaste"

I should like a touch more of the world, the flesh and the devil, for, after all, as your friend Hawkins said, "Somebody must yield to temptation, or the whole thing becomes absurd." If the bottle is your weakness, why not tell the truth and shame the devil? Don't pose as a saint, or you may become one.

Speaking of saints, Her Sanctity of Hinde Street telephoned to me yesterday with the voice of the female sex, which she has now resumed. She has sent me a postcard also to say that Tiresias was wrong when he said the fair sex gets more fun out of fucking than the male. Not a thing to proclaim on a postcard, surely not to write to the lily-pure stripling in the Secret Service.

I apologize.

Last Years

11 St. Leonard's Terrace
TO HIS SISTER MARY   February 22, 1943

We are also getting on as well as can be expected at our age, and under conditions that are not at all uncomfortable. As thee says, our thoughts about old age and death are probably much the same, and there is no need to put them down on paper. On the whole, considering life and all its fantastic passions and real terrors, I am inclined to agree with the septuagenarians who say that old age is the best period of existence, with only one drawback — there is so little of it to enjoy. And when you reach eighty, if you ever reach it, then, they say, the fun begins. It hasn't meant decrepitude for people like Sophocles and Goethe and Voltaire and Wellington; it has been a kind of apotheosis, rather. Take Wellington, for instance, who wrote at eighty-one that he suffered from none of the infirmities of age, except Vanity. And his Vanity was plainly a pleasure, as every day he passed down Piccadilly from Apsley House amid bowed heads and murmurs of wonder and admiration. Has thee heard the story of old Justice Holmes walking at the age of 95 towards the Capitol with another nonagenarian and as a pretty girl passed, sighing "Ah, if I could only be eighty again!"

In planning for my future (tho' I am only 77) I can't decide whether to spend my last days at Weimar in what Carlyle called the mild, divine splendor of Goethe's last golden years — when one can say, as he said to Eckermann, "My remaining days I may now consider as a free gift, since it is of little consequence what I do with them, or whether I do anything."

Reading, however, *Candide* again, and that most divine of all stories, "*La Princesse de Babylone,*" makes me inclined to spend my last days at Ferney, mocking all day with Voltaire at the mad race we belong to. Though Goethe is a god, and Eckermann's *Conversations,* and Lewes'[1] great life of him (the greatest, to my mind, of all biographies) make almost the best of reading, I think I would rather read Voltaire's letters and tales and *Philosophical Dictionary* than spend my days over the *Dichtung und Wahrheit* or the *Wahlverwandtschaften.*

[1] George Henry Lewes (1817–1878), English philosophical writer and critic. His *Life of Goethe* was written in 1855.

A Young Writer of Eighty

11 St. Leonard's Terrace

TO ROSE MACAULAY   December 1945

. . . I enjoy *Time and Tide,* especially on the literary side, which I think Miss [Veronica] Wedgwood edits. She certainly gets hold of clever young writers who write freshly and well. Tell her that there is a young writer under this roof who would be glad and proud to write for her, but fears he is too young, being still early, very early in his eighties.

You kindly came to see him on his 80th birthday and he was very sorry not to be able to see you or anybody else. The truth is that he was very ill and expecting to meet his Creator almost at once. For the present however that encounter has been postponed but it must take place at no very distant date. As he has no theology and the words Sin, Repentance, Atonement, Hell and Heaven haven't the slightest meaning to him, he feels that you, whom he knows to be a profound theologian, might be able (for a suitable fee) to provide him with some robes, or at least rags, of belief to hide his spiritual nakedness on that solemn occasion. How can he best clothe himself with righteousness? Would it do for him to announce himself a Donatist, a Paedobaptist or a Nonjuror? At present two notions appeal to him as rather distinguished — one, to be a Southcottian, versed in the secrets of Joanna Southcott's[1] secret box, or even better, to imitate Joanna's disciple, John Wrol (a good name) the founder of the Christian Israelites who, the D.N.B. tells us, was baptized in running rivers and had himself circumcized in public.

The other scheme is to attain sanctity by renewing the cult of the holy-bearded female saint, St Wilgefortis Uncumber, who grew a great beard and long moustache to protect that jewel which is, or should be, more precious than life to spinster ladies. St Thomas More tells us that St Uncumber was one of the five most popular saints among the Catholics of his time, and that London wives used to celebrate her feast on June 8th every year by bringing to her shrines in Old St Paul's and Westminster Abbey gifts of oats to aid them to get rid of their tiresome husbands.

Don't you think it would be a fashionable and holy thing to revive this cult, and will you help me in it?

In the meantime, I should love to see you. If you would ring up and come to tea any afternoon you will find me here on my deathbed, delighted to see you before I wing my way to Heaven. I have a little Xmas present to give you — the new issue of my *All Trivia*, just reprinted. My life has been spent in mooning over that little book, as it was my fantastic daydream to write a little book which should live on after my own unregretted departure. The new revision contains all those "gossamer touches and last tendernesses" which made the painter Samuel Palmer (Blake's contemporary) unwilling to sell his pictures, which are priceless now.

[1] Joanna Southcott (1750–1814), an English religious fanatic who claimed that she would give birth to a new Prince of Peace. Her followers believed she would return from the dead.

Some Bright Spots

11 St. Leonard's Terrace

TO HUGH TREVOR-ROPER   February 1946

I haven't answered your insults before as (partly [due] to them) I have been in bed with palpitations (if you know what they are) and am likely to spend the rest of my life in that octo-genarially seasonable refuge. Don't pity me, as I am as serene as a lily-pond and perfectly happy. I have hilarious deathbed and cocktail parties every evening from six to seven; only sensitive mourners and earnest-minded legacy hunters are invited; I hope you will come in one or the other, or perhaps both, capacities.

I worry a little about you, as your letter makes me suspect that you are *reading history* which as you know, is never done by history tutors. But they all marry and live in North Oxford. So, I have a lovely wedding present for you, procured by blackmailing the Oxford Press. It can await your nuptials, or you can have it now, if you prefer it. Oxford history tutors, though they never read history, are supposed to keep the standard authorities on their shelves; it helps to keep up the farce. I have some sets of such authorities — Lecky,[1] Freeman, etc. — which it would be wise of you to hyena before [they are] inscribed by others who haven't smelt them out yet. So, I hope to see you soon; I am always in, and welcome visitors, if they will ring me up first.

You ask how I am faring. Well even my dim-age's decline is not without its bright spots to variegate the lily-pond calm I live in. These I will brightly describe:

1. After my impending decease I had a few days of better health and crept downstairs and gave a small tea party —

twelve people, all distinguished and clever, and, like myself, serious thinkers — not a Jezebel or a Goodtime Charlie among them. Rose Macaulay brought Miss Veronica Wedgwood[2] who boasted that she knew you. I liked her extremely and felt that we made friends. She wrote me afterwards a charming letter, expressing her pleasure in making my acquaintance, and saying that she had felt too shy to tell me that her interest in the study of the Seventeenth century was entirely owing to reading my life of Sir Henry [Wotton]. This was the first time since the publication of the book in 1907 that I had heard it sincerely praised, and I felt rewarded for the seven years I had spent in studying original sources, English and foreign archives when

> "From my research the boldest spider fled
> And moths retreated trembling as I read."

II. In contrast to this solitary dewdrop is the drenching of praise I received from America, where the publication of my alembicated and adverbalized new edition of *All Trivia* has raised a storm of applause and the book is selling like hot cakes. The sound of the drums and trumpets reaches me, not unpleasantly, across the Atlantic . . .

III. Owing I think to a mere coincidence, the mention of my name in the *New Statesman*, the *Sunday Times*, and the *Times* itself (see yesterday's leader) has reminded the Jezebels of my existence, and several of the nicer ones have come with gifts down their golden staircases and set a little gossip beside my hilarious deathbed. You once reproved me for speaking with what the Bible calls uncircumcized lips and I tried to change. But both the Jezebels and their wicked gossip have rendered my lips less circumcized than ever.

I'm too old to change my spots and don't really want to change them.

---

[1] William E. H. Lecky (1838–1903), famous for his *History of Rationalism* (1865), *History of European Morals* (1869), and *History of England in the Eighteenth Century* (1878–1890).
[2] Dame Cecily Veronica Wedgwood (1910–   ), English historian known for her books on the seventeenth century. She writes under the name C. V. Wedgwood.

Epitaph

TO HUGH TREVOR-ROPER

11 St. Leonard's Terrace
December 2, 1942

It is kind of you to remember and write to the old derelict I feel myself to be just at present . . . You mock at my loquacity, and seem to think that by the offer of your ear you satisfy the suggestion of that dish of flattery which I was promised for my birthday. Well, that offer I will accept; for appreciation on any terms is a gift which I always welcome. "O power of flattery, how far dost thou extend, and how large are the bounds of thy pleasing jurisdiction!" I cannot help quoting Don Quixote, as I have spent an enchanted week, borne through the days on the eloquent flood [of] this "most lofty, divine and sweet-conceited history," to my mind if not the greatest, at least the most golden of all my golden books; I feel just now as if I should never want another book to read. But I am still too invalidish to write at length except to say that I have found in *Don Quixote* the epitaph which I should like to be mine at my decease:

"Though he achieved not great things, yet did he die in their pursuit."

Index

Beethoven, Ludwig van, 23
Belloc, Hilaire, 78, 78n
Belt, Thomas, 85
Benckendorff, countess, 27, 27n
Bennett, Arnold, 19
Bentley, E. C., 147n
Berenson, Bernard, 54, 138; and Edith Wharton, 93; LPS on memoirs of, 157, 157n; LPS on "smug young" cousin of, 103; on "old age," 49; and Russell compared, 48
Berenson, Mary (née Smith): conversion of LPS, 61; LPS visits I Tatti, 111–15; meets Gertrude Stein, 54; and Whitman, 39–40; on Wilde's life at Posillipo, 102; writings of, 24, 24n
Letters to: 1–2, 7–8, 13–14, 15–16, 24–26, 40–42, 48, 55, 71, 73, 74, 94–95, 96, 100, 113, 116, 121–22, 123–24, 165, 182–83
Berge, Victor, 85
The Bible in Spain (Borrow), 85
bigamy, LPS on, 108
Bigham, Sir Trevor, 98–99
Binyon, Laurence, 154
birdwatching, LPS on, 119
birthday presents, LPS on, 179–80
Blake, William, 11
Blayney, Henry Welladvice, 83
blitzes, LPS on London, 160–62
Bloomsbury, LPS on, 57, 59, 61–62, 115–16
bohemian life, LPS on, 90–91
Book-of-the-Month Club, 142
books recommended by L. P. Smith, 85

bore, LPS on being an old, 166
Borrow, George, 85
Bowen, Elizabeth, 148
Bowen's Court (Bowen), 148
Bridges, Robert, 22, 22n, 142, 170; death of, 69–70; fads of, 65; LPS's admiration for, 65; LPS defends to Trevor-Roper, 78; LPS on mind of, 68; LPS on poetry of, 68–69; memoirs on Dolben, 65–67; and Pronouncing Committee of BBC, 64; and Society for Pure English, 36n, 145; writings of, 69, 130, 131–32n
Letters to: 65–68, 69
Bridges, Mrs. Robert: letter to, 69–70
Broadlands, 100, 100n
Browne, Sir Thomas, 68
Burne-Jones, Lady Georgiana, 138, 138n
Burning of the Leaves (Binyon), 154
Burroughs, John, 40, 40n

Caesar, Julius, 34
Cakes and Ale (Maugham), 86
Candida (Shaw), 108–9
Candide (Voltaire), 183
Caracalla, Emperor, 32
Carlyle, Thomas, 85, 183
Cather, Willa, 58
Catullus, 30
Chanler, Mrs. Winthrop, 95
Chapman, Robert William, 28, 98, 145
Letters to: 98–99, 161–62
"Characters in Fiction" (Woolf), 19, 20, 21
Chekhov, Anton, 125
Chelsea, LPS on, 62–63

Germany, LPS in, 1–7
Gide, André, 142
Gil Blas (Lesage), 72, 84–85
Giotto, 115
The Gods Arrive (Wharton), 75
Goethe, Johann Wolfgang von, 30, 143; LPS on old age of, 183
The Golden Bowl (James), 151
The Golden Grove (Taylor), 140–41
The Golden Grove: Selections from Jeremy Taylor (Smith, L. P.), 139–41
Gooch, George Peabody, 85, 118
Gosse, Sir Edmund, 122, 122n, 138; his library sold, 140–41; LPS on, 140
Greek language, LPS on, 18
Green Mansions (Hudson), 138

halcyon, LPS on, 36
Hall, Joseph (Bishop of Norwich), 140, 141
Hamilton, Lady, 27, 27n
Hannibal, 75n
Harcourt, Brace and Company, 129, 131n
Hardy, Thomas, 23–24, 24n, 86
Harper's, 58
Harrison, Austin, 35
Hazlitt, William, 74
health, LPS on, 172
Hearst publications, 58
Henry James: The Major Phase (Matthiessen), 151, 151n
Hippolytus, legend of, 128
Hogarth Press, 60
Holmes, Justice Oliver Wendell, 103

Horace, 128
Horizon, 152
Horner, Lady, 27, 27n
Housman, A. E., 128
Howells, William Dean, 44n
How Little Logan Was Brought to Jesus (Smith, R.), 61
Hudson, W. H., 138

ideal in literature, 19–21
In the Desert: The Hinterland of Algiers (Phillipps), 138, 138n
In an Enchanted Island: Cyprus (Mallock), 85
invalid, on the delights of being an, 168
Italian, LPS on, 67
Italy, LPS in, 7–8

James, Henry, 20, 78, 86, 115, 151, 169, 170; on Bridges's book on Dolben, 66–67; correspondence with LPS, 130; friendship with LPS, 42–46; and Jane Austen, 28–29; at Lamb House, 43; on the life of the artist, 166; long-tailed similes of, 30; on LPS's gossip, 42; LPS meets, 43; LPS's praise for, 137; meets Santayana, 44; as model for LPS, 127; prefaces of, 76; speaking manner of, 43; suffers strokes, 45; terminal illness and death of, 45–46; on "tragic predicament" of life, 43; on William Du Bois, 58
James, William, 26
Jeanne d'Arc (France), 138
Jews, LPS on, 158–59
Johnson, Samuel, 105

[193]

scholarship, LPS on, 134–36
Scott, Sir Walter, 36, 86;
    Pope-Hennessy biography
    of, 82, 83*n*
Sedgwick, Anne Douglas, 138
Sedgwick, Ellery, 148
    Letter to: 148–49
Sedgwick, Henry, 138
sentences, alternating long
    and short, 16
sermons as literature, 139–41
seventeenth century, LPS on,
    134–35
Shakespeare, William, 25–26,
    135, 181; De Quincey on,
    75; sonnet XXXI quoted,
    170
Shakespeare (Smith, L. P.),
    26
Shaw, Bernard, 64; friendship
    with LPS, 72–73; LPS on
    Candida, 108–9; LPS on
    character of, 73; LPS
    criticism of, 78
Shelley, Percy B., 8, 30
Shenstone, William, 105,
    105*n*
Simpson, Helen, 63
Sing High, Sing Low (Sit-
    well, O.), 152
Sisam, Kenneth, 36, 145–46
Sitwell, Edith, 149, 151; LPS
    praises poetry of, 156–57;
    on middle class vs. aris-
    tocrats, 156; movement to
    nominate as Poet Lau-
    reate, 156–57
Sitwell, Sir George, 149
Sitwell, Sir Osbert, 118, 149,
    150*n*, 151; on Connolly,
    152; on keeping of family
    secrets, 156; LPS on fame
    of, 152
Sitwell, Sacheverell, 149
Smith, Alys. *See* Russell,
    Alys

Smith, Elizabeth, 137, 138*n*
Smith, Hannah (*née*
    Whitall): *The Christian's
    Secret of a Happy Life*,
    LPS on, 130–31; death of,
    163–64; letters of, 131,
    132*n*, 168–69; LPS on,
    130–31
    Letters to: 12–13, 16, 101,
    104, 105, 107–12, 136
Smith, Mary. *See* Berenson,
    Mary
Smith, Logan Pearsall: on
    his achievement, 166–67;
    on aims of life, 171–73;
    aphorisms of, 79–82, 84,
    126; conversion of, 61–62;
    on his correspondence
    with Virginia Woolf,
    130–31; cruising with
    Edith Wharton, 93–97;
    on death of his mother,
    163–64; defense of Jews,
    158–59; epitaph from
    Don Quixote, 187; at
    estate setting of *Mansfield
    Park*, 97–99; on facing
    death, 184–85; feeling for
    words, 173–74; on his
    fiction, 90; on flattery,
    175–77, 179; friendships
    of, 39–87; in Germany as
    student, 1–7; on *The
    Golden Grove*, 139–41;
    on his introspection, 174–
    75; as invalid, 168; in
    Italy, 7–8, 92, 111–15;
    neologisms by, 32–38; on
    new writers, 148–57; on
    old age, 163–87; at Ox-
    ford, 8–14; in Paris, 88–
    91; on reading and writ-
    ing, 15–38; on his 78th
    birthday, 176, 179–80;
    on social life, 100–19; at
    I Tatti, 111–15; on travel,

[197]